The Construction of Social Bonds

NEW HORIZONS IN ORGANIZATION STUDIES

Books in the New Horizons in Organization Studies series make a significant contribution to the study of organizations and the environment and context in which they operate. As this field has expanded dramatically in recent years, the series will provide an invaluable forum for the publication of high-quality works of scholarship and show the diversity of research on organizations of all sizes around the world. Global and pluralistic in its approach, this series includes some of the best theoretical and analytical work with contributions to fundamental principles, rigorous evaluations of existing concepts and competing theories, stimulating debate and future visions.

Titles in the series include:

The Construction of Social Bonds

A Relational Theory of Globalization, Organizations and Society

Göran Ahrne

Professor Emeritus, Department of Sociology, Stockholm University, Sweden

NEW HORIZONS IN ORGANIZATION STUDIES

Edward Elgar
PUBLISHING

Cheltenham, UK • Northampton, MA, USA

Published by
Edward Elgar Publishing Limited
The Lypiatts
15 Lansdown Road
Cheltenham
Glos GL50 2JA
UK

Edward Elgar Publishing, Inc.
William Pratt House
9 Dewey Court
Northampton
Massachusetts 01060
USA

A catalogue record for this book
is available from the British Library

Library of Congress Control Number: 2021946153

This book is available electronically in the **Elgar**online
Sociology, Social Policy and Education subject collection
http://dx.doi.org/10.4337/9781789909456

ISBN 978 1 78990 944 9 (cased)
ISBN 978 1 78990 945 6 (eBook)

Printed and bound by CPI Group (UK) Ltd, Croydon, CR0 4YY

Contents

Preface

It is my firm belief that social theory needs organizational theory more than organizational theory needs social theory. In a global world, it is people's social bonds to their various relationships that are crucial to their ability to act, and crucial for their living conditions. With this book, I want to demonstrate how organizational theory can contribute to the development of a relational social theory.

The idea of social bonds is not a new proposal for a micro–macro link, but it demonstrates the futility of trying to distinguish between the micro and the macro. Several sociologists and other social scientists have strayed into speculation about systems and structures. But to understand the individual's possibilities for action and, above all, the conditions for acting with others, a theory of social bonds and relationships is indispensable. All talk of collective action and various forms of democracy and influence become meaningless if one does not place them in context with the opportunities and limitations that exist in any form of organized action. How can people make joint decisions and how can they get these decisions implemented? Questions about inclusion, exclusion, or recognition are basically questions about organization and social bonds.

In the first chapter, I situate the book's ideas in the social science discussion of micro and macro. Relational sociology has made a key contribution by emphasizing the importance of relationships, but it has gotten itself stuck through its one-sided emphasis on processes and networks. I therefore suggest that we can start again by going back to Max Weber's and Georg Simmel's views on relationships.

In Chapter 2, I develop the theory of social bonds, and in Chapter 3, I discuss the importance of social relationships and examine variations in the construction of social bonds in different types of relationships. Chapter 4 is about organizations as a special kind of relationship, with an analysis of the specialness of a relational organizational theory and how the concepts of traditional organizational theory can be used to develop the idea of social bonds. In Chapter 5, I explain how social bonds give rise to bonded actions. The sixth and last chapter is about globalization and social change – how relationships expand and are held together and how change must be understood in an interplay between inertia and innovation, between old and new relationships.

Writing this book has been very lonely work due to the pandemic. But most of the ideas have been developed together with colleagues and co-authors in various types of relationships (for more details, I refer to the list of references) over many years. My affiliation to Stockholm Centre for Organizational Research (Score) has been decisive for the making of this book. The multidisciplinary research environment at Score is extremely fruitful and stimulating. Drafts of several of the chapters have been discussed at Score seminars. I am also grateful to Score for enabling a qualified language review of my script.

In recent years, I have maintained my contacts with sociology thanks to the participation in two long-running seminars; one with the overall title 'Sociology's current situation' at the Department of Sociology at Uppsala University and the other a seminar series on sociological theory development based at the Norwegian University of Science and Technology.

Göran Ahrne
Knivsta March 2021

1. Why relational sociology?

There has long been an unfortunate tendency in the social sciences to divide society into the micro and the macro. Micro is usually about individuals and actors, whereas macro is described with such terms as 'structure', 'system', or simply 'society'. In sociology, micro and macro are often referred to as occupying separate levels. This way of thinking has locked most of social science research in the area into explanations that either prioritize individuals and their actions or focus on the effects of systems and structures (Ahrne, 1981; Coleman, 1990; Giddens, 1984; Habermas, 1981; Scott, 2021). Norbert Elias (1978) has aptly characterized this stalemate with his contention that 'the individual is at one and the same time surrounded by society yet cut off from it by some invisible barrier' (p. 15).

Many hardcore social theorists emphasize the macro level and the social structure, whereas others, often economists, are critical of those explanations and prefer to address individuals and their preferences. Even laypeople and politicians are usually suspicious of references to structures and systems. As Margaret Thatcher, Prime Minister of the UK from 1979 to 1990, famously maintained, 'there is no such thing as society' (see Outhwaite, 2006, p. 17). On the other hand, many people, including business leaders, sports leaders, and even parents, find it convenient to blame a society that they perceive to be somewhere far away, insisting that it is not their problem, but society's problem.

Many sociologists have devoted themselves to a search for links between the micro and the macro with a variety of proposals. Giddens (1984) has suggested that micro and macro are in fact the same thing seen from different perspectives, whereas Coleman (1990) contends that there is an interaction. Habermas (1981) perceived a system that risks colonization of the lifeworld – the world as experienced by individuals. Although there did seem to be consensus that it was a good idea to conceptualize society as having different levels, these efforts have merely achieved theoretical compromises that fail to abolish the division between micro and macro.

As Collins (1981) has argued, a more fruitful way of understanding the notions of micro and macro is to see them in 'relative terms in both time and space' (p. 987). They can be perceived as a pair of continuous variables, and macrophenomena can be translated into combinations of microevents. Such a translation 'refers to people's repeated behavior in particular places, using particular physical objects, and communicating by using many of the same symbolic expressions repeatedly with certain other people' (p. 994). As Stinchcombe (1985) has stated, 'Macrosociology is sociology about millions of people' (p. 572).

There are many reasons to distrust explanations that unilaterally emphasize society or structure at the expense of the individual. But this does not mean that the focus must be on individual actors. On the other hand, to question the reasonableness of a microperspective does not necessarily mean to ignore people and their choices and values. In recent years, the notion that society is divided into these two levels has been challenged by a relational approach. By looking at people's relationships, we can see how they are recreated or changed through countless everyday events as they move in and out of relationships, their actions reinforcing each other and being captured in relational patterns with long-term effects.

There have been recent discussions about a relational turn in sociology (Prandini, 2015), the purpose of which is to resolve barren antinomies between structure and agency (Crossley, 2011; Mische, 2011). Crossley (2011) assumes that society is 'a process arising between actors' (p. 21). Donati (2011) contends that it is the relationship that constitutes the core and the starting point for an understanding of what society is – that relationships are the 'cells' of society: 'In other words, social relations are those maintaining between agent-subjects that – as such – constitute their reciprocal orientations and actions as distinct from all that characterizes single actors' (p. 60).

BRINGING ORGANIZATIONS BACK IN

My purpose in this book is to demonstrate how theories about organizations can contribute to the development of a relational sociology. There tends to be a large gap between organization theory and more general social theory. Many social theorists prefer to discuss collective action, social movements, institutions, or networks rather than addressing the role of organizations. An analysis of organizations is also lacking in relational sociology. My starting point is that organizations are a type of relationship, and that they should not be understood as situated between micro and macro. Rather, we can understand actions and what we call society *through* relationships. People' actions take place to a large extent in relationships, and society changes as relationships change.

Relationships are held together through social bonds, and there are many kinds of relationships with different characteristics and qualities. In this book, I investigate what happens when one examines organizations from a relational perspective while simultaneously developing a relational sociology from an organizational perspective. Although not usually stated explicitly, much of organization theory is about relationships, and it can be used to develop a relational view of society: Society is not somewhere out there. Society is all around us. There is a tendency in organization theory, however, to see organizations as being at a kind of meso-level between the micro and the macro. We can often hear people talk about ways in which organizations are affected by society and by overall societal processes, without considering that what is 'out there' is, in fact, largely other organizations.

We can only speculate as to why organizational researchers are willing to accept their subordinate role to such a large extent or why other social scientists, such as sociologists and political scientists, overlook the importance of organizations. Perhaps the development of organizational theory in recent years has occurred primarily within business schools and has thus become uncoupled from the development of sociological theories (Besio et al., 2020). Or perhaps it has something to do with the way Max Weber (1930) described rationalized organizations as iron cages characterized by mechanized petrification (pp. 181–182), leading to a disenchantment of the world (Weber, 1946, p. 19). Or perhaps it is simply that organizations appear too obvious and too mundane to fit into an exciting theory of society.

Charles Perrow (2002) is one of the few organizational researchers who has turned against this underestimation of the importance of organizations. One of the most prominent organizational sociologists since the early 1960s, he is perhaps best known for his book on the Harrisburg Nuclear Accident of 1979, *Normal Accidents* (1984). In the introduction to his 2002 book entitled *Organizing America*, he formulates a theory of a society of organizations. He perceives organization as the independent variable and writes that 'the impact of large organizations on society has not been fully appreciated' (p. 10). But we do not even need to enter a discussion about organizations affecting society. They are not reflections of a more general social order (Ahrne et al., 2016). Organizations are society, and society is all around us, both inside and outside organizations.

NEITHER INDIVIDUALS NOR STRUCTURES

But before I begin to discuss how we should be understanding what relationships are and what they consist of, it may be appropriate to mention a few examples of how such concepts as individual and lifeworld or society, structure, and system are defined and how they have been used. When we scrutinize them, we find that they are ambiguous and lacking in clarity.

Individuals

In Anthony Giddens' (1984) theory of structuration, there is a clearly individualistically oriented notion of action: 'Action is a continuous process, a flow,

in which the reflexive monitoring which the individual maintains is fundamental to the control of the body that actors ordinarily sustain throughout their
day-to-day day lives' (p. 9).

But the social context is crucial for the way we should understand individual actions. Max Weber (1968) distinguishes between social and non-social
action. An individual's action is social if it 'takes account of the behavior of
others and is thereby oriented in its course' (p. 4). This orientation towards
other people can apply to the past, present, or future behaviour of others (cf.
Martin, 2009, p. 9). Those to whom the actions are directed can be either an
individual or a larger group of unknown people.

But individual actions are non-social if aimed at inanimate objects. Actions
that cannot primarily be understood as social, Weber (1968) exemplifies with
a common situation: When it starts to rain, a number of individuals independently open their umbrellas (pp. 22–23). These are individual actions that
occur almost simultaneously without any direct connection to each other.

Actions become social when they involve an interaction between acting
people. A strictly individualistic concept of action therefore leads to a mis-
understanding of what happens in society. In a strict sense, a social act is
hardly individual. It presupposes the action of others; a social act remains
incomplete if it is not coordinated with the actions of others. A conversation is
not a conversation if people do not address each other and answer each other's
questions.

We can see social action as a continuous process that goes from individual
to individual; the actions of one individual are complemented by the actions of
another. The individual action loses its meaning if it is not continued by others,
because social actions exceed the physical and mental capacity of individuals.
As further discussed in Chapter 5, they are propagated through interaction and
in relationships.

Lifeworld

The concept of lifeworld comes from phenomenology. Its foremost interpreter
in sociology has been Alfred Schutz (1962). In his presentation, lifeworld is
the part of social reality that an individual encounters in daily life – a part of
society within the reach of each individual (p. 224). A lifeworld is unique to
each individual, and individuals must create their own image and knowledge
of their lifeworld. But it is far from a world that the individual has been
involved in creating. On the contrary. Our lifeworlds existed before we were
born and have come into being as a result of the experiences and actions of
our predecessors 'as an organized world' (Schutz, 1970, p. 72). Lifeworlds
are worlds of multiple realities, pieces of different social sectors that we share
with each other and must adapt to. But for the moment, each of our individual

lifeworlds are ours, and it is up to each of us to give that world meaning and to orient ourselves in it.

The multiple realities of the lifeworld and its objects can in another, perhaps gloomier phenomenological interpretation be described as a practico-inert field (Sartre, 1976). This field can be seen as an objectified practice. It is through the mediation of the objects in the field of the practico-inert – activities and structures inherited from ancestors – that different lifeworlds meet. In this way, human relations are arranged in seriality (pp. 259–261). People share something in common that simultaneously separates them. The connections between individuals are negatively determined through their links with objects in a practico-inert field.

The various objects in a lifeworld offer resistance. As Foucault (1979) would have it, power is exercised in lifeworlds. But an individual's movements in the lifeworld are also 'modifying or changing its objects and their mutual relationships' (Schutz, 1970, p. 73). To the extent that individuals have the opportunity to choose between exit and voice in different contexts (Hirschman, 1970), they can influence the objects around which the lifeworld revolves.

A lifeworld does not seem to exist separate from a social structure, then. Rather, the opposite. Lifeworlds are in the midst of these structures and consist of each individual's way of moving and interpreting them. From a lifeworld perspective, individuals consciously or unconsciously shape these structures through their bodily movements and in the choice between exit and voice. Micro and macro are intimately connected. It is in lifeworlds, on the ground, that things are determined.

Society

The establishment of the idea of society as beyond and partly separate from humans was a prerequisite for the emergence of a social science distinct from such other disciplines as philosophy, psychology, and biology (Tilly, 1984). The idea of society demonstrated something that ruled and had power over people without being a divine or princely force. In everyday language, the term 'society' is used in a variety of contexts. It can refer to a state, or from an individual viewpoint, it can stand for people who are unknown except perhaps as TV personalities. One's immediate surroundings or lifeworld are rarely seen as society.

Roughly speaking, one can distinguish between two fundamentally different ways of summarizing what the term 'society' stands for; it 'has a useful double meaning' (Giddens, 1984, p. xxvi). In the most common and conventional use of the term, various scholars have differentiated among various societies and suggest that *a society constitutes a delimited geographical unit separate from other such units* (Parsons, 1951; cf. Giddens, 1984; Tilly, 1984). According to

Talcott Parsons' (1966) functionalist theory, a society is a collective that constitutes a social system. What makes it a society is its relative self-sufficiency (p. 9). In practice, the use of the term 'society' in this sense equates it with a country or a state, with each country being perceived as a separate society. This view has been heavily criticized, not least in light of a growing awareness of globalization. Charles Tilly (1984) was early in advancing this critique:

> All of the standard procedures for delineating societies run into severe trouble when the time comes either to check the clarity and stability of the social boundaries thus produced or to describe the coherent structures and processes presumably contained within those boundaries. (p. 23)

From a global perspective, only a society that encompasses the whole world has fully unambiguous boundaries (Outhwaite, 2006, p. 52).

Even as globalization processes erode the independence of states, they are contributing to a fragmentation of these so-called societies. But as Udehn (2016) suggested, the conclusion must be that these are neither sufficiently integrated nor sufficiently delimited from the outside world to be considered social systems.

Tilly (1984) concluded his critique of the idea of conceptualizing society as a thing apart, as having a specific spatial delimitation, by suggesting that instead of seeing societies as different autonomous systems, we should apply the idea of multiple social relationships, 'some quite localized, and some worldwide in scale' (p. 25).

The second meaning of the term 'society' is to see it as *the sum of all social relations and interaction among people*. This view of society was, in fact, the most common one before the breakthrough of structural functionalism in the 1940s. The classical sociologist who gave the most pregnant expression to this interpretation of society was Georg Simmel, who was active at the end of the 19th and the beginning of the 20th century (Frisby & Sayer, 1986). Without abandoning the idea of something social that influences and can explain human actions, Simmel proceeded from these actions. Society is everywhere 'where a number of human beings enter into interaction and form temporary or permanent unity' (Simmel, quoted from Frisby & Sayer, 1986, p. 59).

For Simmel (1909), society was an abstraction that expressed the forces generated in interactions between people when they socialize and cooperate or compete and fight with each other. The concept of society covers two meanings:

> first, the complex of associated individuals, the socially formed human material, as the full historical reality has shaped it. 'Society' is, second, the sum of those forms of relationship by virtue of which individuals are changed into 'society' in the former sense. (p. 301)

Structure

A common expression of the micro–macro dichotomy is to talk about actor and structure. Is there a difference between society and structure? Perhaps it can be said that the structure is the skeleton of a society (Scott, 2021). But, as with society, there is no agreement on what structure stands for. According to Joas and Knöbl (2009), structure has become 'something of a jack-of-all trades, deployed to a diverse array of ends in every imaginable context, which is precisely why it is rarely defined in any detail' (p. 343).

The concept of structure is a relatively new element in social theory; it was not until the 1960s that it began to be widely used. It was first introduced in anthropology and came to replace the concept of function (Lizardo, 2010). Before long, structure became established as a cornerstone of social science vocabulary: 'from being an unwieldy and unevenly used abstraction', structure became a 'seemingly obligatory part of the vocabulary of contemporary sociologists' (p. 653).

Structure has been used primarily as an analytical tool in anthropology, but in Anthony Giddens' version, structure became an ontological concept, an assumption about the nature of social reality (Lizardo, 2010). According to Giddens (1984), however, this social reality, in turn, consists of rules and resources: 'Structure as recursively organized sets of rules and resources, is out of time and space, save as instantiations and coordination as memory traces, and is marked by an absence of the subject' (p. 25). He also contended that institutions have a place in this structural concept: 'Those practices which have the greatest time-space extension within such totalities can be referred to as institutions' (p. 22).

A social structure that consists of combinations of rules, resources, and institutions is far from a monolithic solid block that forces social life into certain definite forms, but rather a web of relationships with different extents and boundaries in time and space. Rather than referring to structure in a definite form as the cause of certain phenomena or behaviours, we must be able to say what that structure comprises. And if we address this issue in terms of changing such structures, it may rather mean changing rules or institutions. In his book, *Social Structures*, John Levi Martin (2009) developed an approach based on the notion that social structures are results and effects rather than causes. He was interested in the emergence of structures and rejected the idea that social structures could explain regularities in social action. For Martin, structures are a form of 'patternings of relationships' (p. 3). If one is to mention structures, then, it is as the effects of human actions rather than as something that explains them.

Society Is All Around Us

The idea of societies defining self-sufficient systems is clearly outdated. The world is not divided into a number of separate societies. Yet we cannot say that there is no such thing as society. To think of society is to think of people. Without people, there is no society; and without society, there are no people. Society is not far away; society is not the others; society is all around us, as manifested in our interactions and our relationships.

When we think of people and society, perhaps we should distinguish between individuals and human beings. Each individual is distinct from every other individual, but a human being is one of many. Individuals have difficulty with relationships. A basic idea for Simmel (1910) was that 'the individual soul cannot be inserted into an order without finding itself at the same time in opposition to it' (p. 384). But for human beings, relationships are a matter of course.

As social beings, people are not individuals; they are siblings, parents, friends, cousins, neighbours, citizens, colleagues, members, volunteers, patients, supporters, prisoners, students, team-mates, or tenants. Being a sibling provides different conditions for a relationship than being a member of an organization, a patient, or a prisoner does. Many people are in relationships that are not characterized by cooperation or common agreements, rather the opposite; they are competitors, rivals, enemies, or opponents. People live their lives in relationships, are born into relationships, sometimes leaving relationships if they can, but looking for new relationships. Changing society means changing relationships.

WHAT ARE RELATIONSHIPS?

Many scholars who write about relational sociology emphasize that social analysis should be based on interaction between people. But there is a crucial difference between interaction and a relationship. Relationships are developed through repeated interaction; a relationship creates opportunities to meet the same people on several occasions. According to Crossley (2011), a relationship consists of 'the sedimented past and projected future of a stream of interaction' (p. 35). It is developed through experiences from previous interactions, influencing and shaping a continued interaction. A relationship can be strengthened or weakened through interaction. Each relationship has a special 'temporal code' (Donati, 2011, p. 89), a history, but its continuation cannot be taken for granted.

But a relationship is more than repeated interaction. Meeting a person again, hanging out, or doing something together can happen by chance; people may meet again because they live close to each other or take the same route to work.

In order for a relationship to arise and be maintained, something more must be created – something that constitutes the conditions for continued contacts, some type of communication that can make it possible to meet again or keep in touch without any direct interaction. The bonds with which a relationship is held together and the conditions they create are crucial for an analysis and understanding of their meaning and how they work. They are needed for the relationship to continue, but they also create a certain distance; bonds hold people both together and apart and sometimes simultaneously. In general terms, relational sociologists such as Prandini (2015) refer to these enabling conditions as ties or building blocks. A recurring theme is that relationships are 'constituted by story' (White, 1992, p. 67; cf. Tilly, 2002, chapter 3). Crossley (2011) suggests that we 'tell stories about our relationships' (p. 36). It can also be about 'conversational situations' (Mische & White, 1998). Some authors emphasize transactions as elements that bind relationships together (Dépelteau, 2008; Tilly, 2005a). Others note that relationships require negotia-tions between those involved, for relationships must be constantly maintained (Crossley, 2011). All these proposals can be understood as communicative events. Different forms of communication shape, stabilize, or change rela-tional expectations (Fuhse, 2015).

Yet, relational sociologists have not come far in explaining the conditions under which it is possible to create relationships, and how they arise and are reproduced. The proposals that have been made – story-telling, transactions, and negotiations – are vague. And there are a lack of decisive insights into the way relationships are created – possibilities for inclusion and who may or may not participate, for example. I discuss this issue in the next chapter and develop a way of defining the terms and conditions for establishing relationships more closely, with the help of social bonds.

Why have relational sociologists been so vague in explaining the elements that hold relationships together? Probably because the area has been developed by sociologists who focus on studies of networks. Many of their main ideas have emerged in the academic circle of Harrison White and Charles Tilly of Columbia University, which is why the perspective is sometimes referred to as the New York School (Fuhse, 2015; Mische, 2011; Prandini, 2015). But there are several other roots. In most of the contributions, however, relationships are equated with networks. Ann Mische's (2011) article on the emergence of a relational sociology, entitled 'Relational sociology, culture and agency', is included in the *SAGE Handbook of Social Network Analysis*. She emphasizes that relational sociology has developed from general insights based on network analysis. And even those who do not directly have their intellectual roots in the New York School seem to equate relationships with networks, as evident in Crossley's (2011) statement: 'relationships are real and the social world com-prises actors-in-relationship – in networks' (p. 23; cf. Donati, 2011, pp. 92–94;

Fuhse, 2015). The fact that culture constitutes a dominant research interest in relational sociology is probably another reason for the underdevelopment of the notion of what constitutes relational building blocks.

The idea that organizations can be understood as relationships rarely exists within this school, although Tilly (2002) mentioned organizations even as he argued for a relational perspective (p. 73), and Crossley (2015) advanced the idea that corporate actors such as trade unions, companies, or authorities can be seen as actors in a relational sociology (p. 66).

In addition to the criticism of the division of society into a macro and a micro level, there has been a tendency in relational sociology to emphasize processes at the expense of structure or substance. In the introduction to his article, 'Manifesto for a relational sociology', Mustafa Emirbayer (1997) held forth that there is a contradiction in sociology between 'conceiving of the social world as consisting primarily in substances or processes, in static "things" or in dynamic, unfolding relations' (p. 281).

There may be tensions between process and substance, but these notions are hardly mutually exclusive. Substances arise from processes, and processes need some substance in which to develop. Not everything can flow; water must have something in which to flow. It is sometimes said that one cannot descend into the same river twice. Yet we know that rivers are ancient.[1] Rivers consist not only of water, but also of riverbeds, beaches, and their deltas. And it is claimed that Heraclitus did not say exactly that one cannot descend into the same river twice, but rather said something to the effect of 'Around those who descend into the same rivers, new water is constantly flowing.' Rather than being contradictions, then, substance and process condition each other.

Relationships can be understood as a flow of repeated interaction that changes for each occasion of interaction. But there must still be something that holds the relationship together in order for it to continue. A relationship needs substance and form. As Vandenberghe (2018) noted, 'What appears as a solid particle is also a wave; structure is also process' (p. 47). The distinction between structure and process is temporal. In identifying boundary specification as one of the biggest problems for a relational analysis, Emirbayer (1997) indirectly admits that processes need a form, 'moving from flows to transactions to clearly demarcated units of study, from continuity to discontinuity' (p. 303).

Network-inspired relational sociology has provided a foundation to stand on and support the fruitfulness of a relational approach to society. But its focus on networks and processes runs the risk of leading it into a dead end. Not all relationships are networks. If that were the case, there would be no reason to refer to networks; it would be enough to comment on relationships. In order to develop a relational social science that includes organizations and other types of relationships, we must continue along a different path. Maybe it is a good idea to go back a bit and follow a track from Max Weber. He did not have to struggle with micro and macro; nor did he have to deal with networks.

Relationships According to Weber

I previously discussed how Weber (1968) distinguished between social and non-social action in his introduction to *Economy and Society*. What makes an individual's action social is that it is directed at someone or some other people. Weber's view of social relationships relates to his description of social action and follows directly on the analysis of social action. Relationships arise through people's mutual social actions. A social relationship, according to Weber, is the behaviour of a plurality of actors for whom 'the action of each takes account of that of the others and is oriented in these terms' (p. 26).

Social relationships can be based upon diverse things, from friendships and sexual relationships on the one hand, to political relationships and economic transactions on the other. But every relationship revolves mainly around a specific content. Moreover, they can be based upon mutual solidarity and appreciation or upon hostility and conflict (Weber, 1968, p. 27).

Relationships are shaped in a variety of ways. Some, which Weber referred to as 'associative relationships', are based upon decided agreements and can often be about different types of financial transactions. He also identified 'communal relationships', based upon traditional or emotional grounds. Weber noted that these different aspects of a relationship can overlap in more permanent social relationships between the same persons. In such relationships, emotional values may exceed pure utility aspects (p. 41). But not all relationships remain long lasting. A social relationship may be of a 'very fleeting character' or of 'varying degrees of permanence' (p. 28).

Perhaps Weber's (1968) most significant distinction was between open and closed relationships. In open relationships, it is possible in principle for anyone to participate, and there is nothing to stop those who want to join. He mentioned religious movements and market relationships as examples of open relationships. But a relationship is closed, he contended, 'so far as, according to its subjective meaning and its binding rules participation of certain persons is excluded, limited or subjected to conditions' (p. 43). The fact that a relationship is closed, however, does not imply that individual members do not come and go, merely that involvement is not unconditional and open to everybody. In the long run, there is a tendency in most relationships to move from openness to closedness. It does not matter if they can be seen as associative or communal. But this change often occurs gradually, and there are many variations between openness and closure, ranging from exclusive clubs or the audience that bought tickets to a concert to a political meeting to which as many people as possible are welcome (p. 45).

Immediately following his analysis of social relationships, Weber (1968) moved on to the concept of organization. An organization is the most typical example of a closed social relationship, but not all closed relationships are organizations. Another example is kinship. The fact that a social relationship is closed, however, is not enough for it to be seen as an organization. In an organization, closure is linked to authority and rules. A closed social relationship is regarded as an organization only 'when its regulations are enforced by specific individuals' (p. 48). The existence of an organization 'is entirely a matter of the presence of a person in authority' (p. 49). This authority is expressed in orders or rules. Thus, in Weber's view, an organization, apart from being a type of closed social relationship, also requires orders, rules, and some form of authority.

*   *   *

In the following three chapters, I develop the analysis of social relationships. In Chapter 2, I address the ways in which social relationships are constructed using social bonds, which can be fashioned in different ways. Relationships can be more or less organized. In Chapter 3, I demonstrate variations between relationships that have no organization and relationships such as family, friendship, gangs, and social movements that may be partially organized. That chapter begins with a comparison between the idea of social relationships and similar concepts, such as group, collective action, network, and figuration. In Chapter 4, I analyse formal organizations as social relationships, and demonstrate how a number of traditional concepts in organizational theory can be given a relational interpretation. In the two concluding chapters, I return to the question of individual and society, but from a relational perspective. Chapter 5 highlights a relational concept of action: bonded actions. And in Chapter 6, I show how social change and globalization can be understood by examining social relationships.

NOTE

1. 'I've known rivers:
   Ancient dusky rivers.' (Langston Hughes)

2.   Social bonds

Bonds hold things together. When we talk about social bonds, we are talking about people who are bound together in social relationships. But bonds are not merely about people sticking together. When objects are tied together in special ways, something new can be created; a pile of logs can become a raft, and a number of horses can be linked together to pull heavy carriages. Through the way in which social bonds are connected, something new can be created, even though the individuals do not change. They are still discernible parts of a relationship; the only difference is the bonds that link them together. This bonding can make their personal qualities work together to support or complement each other.

Bonds can be constructed in different ways and of different materials, depending on their function and what is being held together. Different purposes require different forms of bonds: if they are to be as strong as possible or to be flexible; if they are expected to last for a long or short time; if they are soft enough that they do not hurt those held together or hard enough to resist attempts at dissolving them.

The concept of social bonds is not common in the social science literature. Charles Tilly (1998), who emphasized the importance of bonds (p. 21), has provided no clues as to how we can proceed to analyse different forms of social bonds. In criminology, a theory of social bonds has been developed to explain why many people never commit crimes: a negative relationship between the strength of the bond that binds those individuals to society and the likelihood that they will commit criminal acts (Hirschi, 1969). German–US sociologist Werner Stark (1980) has written an extensive work in several volumes entitled *The Social Bond: An Investigation into the Bases of Law-Abidingness*. As the title suggests, Stark contends that social bonds are also about the individual's relationship to society at large, although Stark prefers the concept of community. For Stark, the social bond creates 'out of many individuals one community' (p. 23). He emphasizes that social bonds do not arise through human instincts; nor are they developed spontaneously. Rather, they emerge through 'the efforts of men dwelling side by side to solve their personal life problems' (p. 22).

When the term *social bond* is used in the social science literature, it seems to be about bonds to society. But if there is no society? Then human bonds are not anchored; they get stuck in nothingness. Instead, we have to think that people are bound together with other people in relationships, and that each person is part of a number of relationships.

The same relationship can be held together by a number of social bonds with different design, durability, and elasticity. It is necessary, therefore, to distinguish between social bonds and social relationships. A social relationship can continue to exist even though some of its bonds are dissolved – if some of the members quit. And social bonds can last even though a relationship is dissolved – if a family is dissolved by the parents divorcing, the bonds between siblings and between the respective parents and child remain.

In analysing the way social bonds are created, it is tempting to think that they are always established between individuals; but in many cases one of these individuals can be acting on behalf of a collective. Social bonds are linked to specific individuals. They are personal (cf. Martin, 2009, p. 340). When a person leaves a bond, the bond dissolves; that bond no longer exists, and the person cannot be replaced.

In this chapter, we take a closer look at social bonds before discussing social relationships in Chapter 3.

THE SIGNIFICANCE OF SOCIAL BONDS

The fact that individuals are connected through social bonds does not mean that they become less human or lose their free will. Social bonds do not turn people into puppets ruled by higher powers. A social bond does not prevent people from having their own opinions, but it can influence and control when and how those opinions are expressed. As Stark (1980) noted, social bonds are necessary to help solve their problems. People are so dependent on others that they accept their social bonds even though they may sometimes oppose or resist the way the bonds are formed.

People have few opportunities to decide on their own or choose their social bonds. They can choose the jobs they want to apply for or who they would like for friends, but for a bond to be established, someone else must recognize it; one must be accepted or selected to a bond. With the exception of innate social bonds such as those of citizenship or family, others are the ultimate deciders of the bonds to which a person can belong.

In some cases, however, people may decide for themselves to establish a social bond. A person could acquire citizenship in a state by investing more money in that country or join a voluntary association in which membership can be acquired merely by registering and paying a membership fee. But this is far from the case for all associations, and members can usually be excluded if they behave in a way that goes against the association's statutes. But with the exception of these cases, people have little opportunity to determine their social bonds independently – unless they do it through force or coercion, against the will of the other person, as in kidnapping.

The fact that people are not usually able to make the final decisions about their social bonds does not mean that these bonds are necessarily entered into involuntarily. But even if both parties establish them voluntarily, they are not necessarily equal. It is not uncommon for social bonds to be asymmetrical relationships in which one party is more dependent on one bond than the other, and that the bonds are based on or even obtain their strength from the fact that one party has power resources that affect and maintain the mutual recognition of the bond.

Each individual has a unique set of social bonds, and it is through these bonds that an individual becomes a social being. How their bonds arise and are shaped is key to an individual's position among other individuals in society. An individual's set of social bonds explains a great deal of that individual's behaviour.

Social bonds provide both opportunities and limitations. For an individual to have a social bond means that there is another person waiting for, recognizing, and knowing that individual. An individual who is not personally recognized may be identified by a pass, passport, other ID document, or such physical characteristics as fingerprints or facial recognition. But the fact remains that a social bond is personal – that there are expectations of the person and that someone cares whether the person shows up or not. Being tied into a social bond is both a limitation of one's freedom of movement (the inability to choose where to go at that time) and a restriction of freedom of choice. Yet, without social bonds, people have nowhere to stay. The opposite of being bound is not to be free, but to be excluded.

And every individual has a limited number of social bonds, which implies that most people most of the time are excluded from almost all existing relationships. As Niklas Luhmann (2018) stated, 'Exclusion is therefore the normal, inclusion the exception' (p. 323).

People are well aware of their social bonds; they provide context, meaning, and identity. The importance of social bonds was expressed in a newspaper interview with a young woman. She was asked, 'What is the best thing about being you?' And she answered, 'It's enough that I get to have the people I have around me. To be me is to be with them.'

If we walk around a larger city, we see many individuals walking or travelling on their own. They often seem to be in a hurry and to look lonely. But the vast majority are on their way somewhere, to a place where someone waits for them. Social bonds are threads in people's lifeworlds, and the relationships to which the bonds are connected can be understood as a web of multiple realities. Many bonds are so obvious that they do not appear as bonds; they are taken for granted. It is only when a person's movements lead outside the habitual lifeworld or if the lifeworld changes drastically that the significance of bonds or the lack of bonds can become apparent – when there is nowhere to go and bonds dissolve without being immediately replaced by others.

Although not impossible, it is difficult to imagine a person without any social bonds, a person who is orphaned, stateless, without relatives or friends, who is unemployed, and belongs to no association. There are such people on earth today, however, and no one knows their number. Their lives do not represent total freedom. They represent total vulnerability.

For most people, social bonds are a matter of course. When we are born, a biological bond is transformed into a social bond. And through birth or adoption, we are likely to be bonded not only to our parents, but also to siblings, to other relatives, and to a state. The number of and our dependence upon social bonds varies with age. Childhood bonds are few but strong. The dependence, but not the number, may decrease during adolescence, even as new bonds, new friends, contacts of various kinds are created. But the old bonds remain, even if they are not as prominent in everyday life.

Different bonds have different relevance for the individual; some have great significance in everyday life and for the way people move in their lifeworlds, whereas others, like citizenship, have less everyday significance but all the more importance for one's entire life situation. The more bonds a person is bound by, the greater the fragmentation of everyday life, which can create conflict and tension between demands and expectations of the various relationships.

That the same individual is simultaneously bound by a number of social bonds with different other individuals or collectives requires certain characteristics of the bonds. People are not literally chained to each other; they must be able to move in and out of their bonds. The bonds must be able to be loosened without breaking and be reconnected. It is especially the opportunity to return or the promise to return that is the basis of all social bonds. The bonds remain, even though it may be a long time between occasions when they are connected. This necessary flexibility of most social bonds allows them to appear less tangible and crucial than they are.

There is currently a great deal of talk about individualization (Udehn, 2007) – the idea that individuals are independent actors. This notion is based on the proposition that people in pre-modern times (when being indefinite) were more dependent on their families and relatives than are people today. It could be that fewer but stronger and tighter social bonds once bound people, at least in large parts of Europe and North America (cf. Simmel, 1964, pp. 148–150). But to describe this phenomenon as individualization is deceptive. Rather, social bonds have changed character, having increased in flexibility while increasing in number. The fact that most of us carry mobile phones wherever we go is a sign of our dependence on social bonds more than it is a sign of our freedom.

THE PERCEPTION OF OTHERS' SOCIAL BONDS

Social bonds are important not only for those who are directly part of a relationship. In the introduction to his book, *The Presentation of Self in Everyday Life*, Erving Goffman (1959) wrote: 'When an individual enters the presence of others, they commonly seek to acquire information about him' (p. 1). This applies not least to an individual's social bonds.

In our encounters with other people, our interest usually goes beyond them as individuals. We want to know about their social bonds, with whom they are familiar, if they are married or in a stable relationship, if they have siblings, who their coworkers, friends, and acquaintances are, and where they are from. Such knowledge has many practical advantages; it says something about what we can expect from others when we meet them. It matters, because it will determine what we say or do not say and what further relationships we can expect to have with each other.

There are situations in which people's bonds can even be more important than the individuals themselves. When being interviewed by a journalist, for instance, it is probably more important to know which news medium the journalist represents than it is to know about the journalist as a person. But the one does not necessarily exclude the other.

Old, dissolved bonds may also be of interest to others: Where has the person been employed, and to whom has the person been married? Even previous bonds, such as love or political relationships, can be obstacles to making new bonds.

People are treated differently depending on their social bonds. This applies not only to such intimate relationships as love and friendship, but also to workplace or political relationships. Politicians from the same party treat each other differently than do politicians from other parties. And people are treated differently at state borders depending on their citizenship.

Not knowing another person's social bonds creates uncertainty; one does not know what resources that person can mobilize in the future, making it more difficult to assess the consequences of the way a meeting proceeds. Even when people make good impressions, it is natural to wonder if they have nice friends, rich parents, suitable contacts, powerful protectors, or even a capital of violence to mobilize. In many contexts, it is expected that people with whom we are interacting are parts of bonds, and that other members can be consulted if one is treated badly. Who is the person's manager, team leader, or parent? Who can take responsibility for the way that person behaved?

How do we learn about a person's social bonds? How much can we ask people we meet for the first time about their bonds? The answer varies with the situation. One can generally assume that it is neither pleasant nor polite to ask about such things directly. People often want to appear as independent individuals, although there are some who like to brag about their solid ancestry or their important contacts. In a job interview, however, it is more legitimate to inquire about social bonds – by asking direct questions and requesting references, for example.

It is possible through conversation to discover a person's bonds by asking them where they live, where they went to school, and so on. But it is more difficult to ask if they are married or have children. Over time, though, it is possible to gain more knowledge about the other person's social bonds gradually; getting to know a person is getting to know their social bonds. But it is also possible to gain knowledge about a person's social bonds in advance by asking others or by searching the Internet, LinkedIn, Facebook, and Google – at least after the first meeting.

There can also be clues about a person's social bonds. In many countries, married people are expected to wear a ring or two; that is far from a sure sign, however, and it provides no information about the person to whom the individual is married. Furthermore, many people with stable relationships do not wear rings.

Fortunately for people trying to glean information about others, it is not uncommon for individuals to signal some of their social bonds, more or less discretely with various symbols. They may be wearing a uniform or dressed in a way that marks an affiliation. A politically active person may wear a badge; a football supporter may wear a badge or scarf in the club's colours. Conference participants often wear badges with their name and organizational affiliation clearly displayed. Gang affiliation can be marked with tattoos. These are all ways of conveying information to others about our social bonds.

In some contexts, when we encounter new people in a slightly larger gathering, they can signal how they belong together and in what way. Goffman (1971, chapter 5) calls these signal *tie-signs*: When those who belong together show it through a special intimacy, by touching each other, holding hands, or speaking to each other in a warm tone of voice.

When people are introduced by first and last name, the last name may provide an idea of their bonds, whether kinship, ethnicity, or marriage. Sometimes we are introduced to a person by someone we know, which immediately provides a clue, particularly if the introducer provides information about their bond: 'I'd like you to meet my colleague from Canada' or 'This is my sister's husband, Jon Norberg.'

WHAT ARE SOCIAL BONDS MADE OF?

Social bonds are formed through communication. Some form of communication precedes any inclusion in a relationship (Schoeneborn et al., 2014), the only exception being a new-born baby. Communication can be considered an action or a transaction between two parties. Communicative actions are prerequisites for establishing and maintaining relationships and apply to things that the relationship is about. Relational communication is primarily linguistic, whether oral and written, but it can also take place through 'non-linguistic behaviour' (Winch, 2008, p. 120). Relational communication is mainly action oriented, although the direct connection between talk and action is not a given. It is not self-evident that all linguistic actions are accompanied by corresponding bodily actions; neither is it obvious that people do as they themselves say they should do or as others tell them to do.

Both the content of a communication and its sources can have different character. In further analysis of how social bonds are formed, I distinguish among three main types of communication: the institutional communication, decisions, and reciprocity. These three communication types differ in the origin of the communicated message and how it, in turn, affects how the message is conveyed.

Institutional communication mediates a stable, routine-reproduced pattern of behaviour, combined with norms and conceptions that are taken for granted (Jepperson, 1991). Institutions develop slowly (Czarniawska, 2009) and are difficult to change (North, 1998). They emerge in a historical process of interaction and habitualization. Institutionalization begins when two or more individuals interact repeatedly and begin to develop a common understanding of what they are doing and how to do it; their interactions become predictable, and they note, 'There we go again' (Berger & Luckmann, 1991, p. 75).

The origin of the content of institutional communication is not clear; it has emerged gradually and has come to be taken for granted as something that is undoubtedly true and correct, such as norms and customs. The message is this: 'That is how things should be done. This is how it should be.' Fashion and trends are also forms of institutional communication about what is the right thing to do during a certain period and in a certain situation.

Institutions can be used for many purposes in the construction of social bonds; they are ready made, easy to use, and have strong legitimacy. Institutional components can be expected to produce strong bonds; they are reliable and work in many contexts, but they are often rather general and lack precision.

Decisions are a form of communication connected with organization. As Luhmann (2018) put it, 'organizations arise and reproduce themselves when decisions are communicated' (p. 41). Decisions have a wide range, in that they can be disseminated both orally and in writing, and they do not require direct interaction between sender and recipient. A decision has a clear origin; a decision always has a sender; a message about a certain decision refers to a decision maker, who has the responsibility for the decision (Brunsson, 2007, pp. 18–19). A decision maker can be one individual, but it can also be a board or a larger democratic assembly.

Unlike institutions, decisions are not taken for granted; a decision is often a surprise, and those affected by the decision wonder what it will be, because, and as Luhmann (2018) noted, 'Decisions mark a difference between past and future' (p. 43). Decisions are choices among options; the decision maker could have chosen another path. Decisions are often contested: Why was not another option chosen, another decision made? Individuals who are dissatisfied with a decision know to whom they can direct their complaints or protests.

Decisions are the most significant form of communication for the construction of social bonds in organizations. But individuals can also make common decisions regarding their relationships, which they communicate to other people and organizations – that they have decided to become a couple and get married, for example.

In the beginning of their book, *Organizations*, James March and Herbert Simon (1958) emphasize that in comparison to other influence processes, the most salient quality of organization is its specificity; decisions may contain great detail (p. 3). When decisions are used for the construction of social bonds, they must be decided anew for each new bond. Decisions can be adapted to new circumstances, but they are not taken for granted and can often be questioned. Moreover, they are not as stable as institutional elements; they can be changed with new decisions.

Reciprocity is a third type of communication in the development of social bonds. It rests upon the implicit turn-taking that occurs between parties. Reciprocity can be a factor in several types of social bonds: It is 'a plastic filter, capable of being poured into the shifting crevices of social structures and serving as a kind of all-purpose moral cement' (Gouldner, 1959, pp. 249–250).

The model for an understanding of reciprocity is gift giving, which has been analysed in Marcel Mauss' (2002) classic essay. Giving a gift, inviting someone to a party, or offering a service to someone can be interpreted as an attempt to form a bond. Reciprocity cannot be decided upon and organized; there is no explicit agreement between the person who gives a gift and the one who receives it. But there is an unspoken expectation that the gift or invitation or service should be returned in kind. Gifts are not immediately reciprocated, however. There is a period of indeterminacy, and one cannot even take for granted that the gift or invitation will be reciprocated (Gouldner, 1959). Perhaps the receiver is not able to reciprocate or does not want to reciprocate.

Moreover, reciprocity is about power; an invitation or a gift is a challenge to the receiver to reciprocate in an appropriate manner. Even if gifts or invitations have been reciprocated a number of times, the indeterminacy remains. But every time a gift or an invitation is reciprocated, it represents recognition of a continuation of a bond.

There are other forms of interpersonal communication less central to our discussion – gossip, for example. Gossip refers to the stories that people tell about each other – anything that someone has seen or heard about someone else. Gossip often contains an evaluation of specific persons and their actions or achievements (Burt, 2005, p. 105), whether negative or positive (Grosser et al., 2010). Gossip is a central feature in many networks, and opportunities to exchange gossip are central to the cohesion of networks (Elias & Scotson, 1994, chapter 7).

WHAT CAN SOCIAL BONDS DO?

No bonds are required merely to interact with other people. It is enough that two or more people happen to meet in some context in a specific place. But with the help of social bonds, people can keep in touch with each other without having to meet. Bonds create conditions for repeated interaction, repeated contact, or communication. Social bonds transcend time and space, creating cohesion that does not depend on meeting at a certain place at a certain time in person.

There can be many reasons for people wanting to keep in touch. They know enough about each other that they can continue their interactions where they left off. They may have a common history, based upon emotions, interests, common frames of reference, or mutual understanding, or they simply know that they complement each other and can do things together; they know who is good at what. And people may want to keep in touch for reasons ranging from personal relationships like love or friendship to the bonds between employees of a company or even citizens of the same state. Social bonds unite them and distinguish them from others.

Over time, if the bonds remain, they may be subjected to stress and wear out. Things are happening all around them, and communication must be kept up to date and renewed. As Ostrom has suggested, a theory of what social bonds can do must be based on 'realistic assessments of human capabilities and limita-tions' (1990, p. 23).[1] Strong emotions are not enough to maintain relationships.

We can essentially distinguish five things that social bonds do. (1) They delimit and include the people involved in a relationship, (2) they convey and express the expectations that those involved have of each other, (3) they make it possible to discover and assess what the other person is doing, (4) they gradually adapt and correct the relationship (or, alternatively, cut the bonds), and (5) they create patterns for communication – how their communication should be handled and in what order they should communicate (cf. Ahrne & Brunsson, 2019, p. 7).

Affiliation

In order for a relationship to be established, the people who are to be covered by a bond must be distinguished and identified, and they can no longer be anonymous. It is not enough that they recognize each other if they happen to meet. The bond is meant to create opportunities to keep in touch. They need to know something more than a name about each other – an address, an e-mail address, a phone number, information about where they can meet on certain days or times.

That a bond is established depends on a hope or a plan for continuation, but in addition to the people involved meeting more than once, the time perspective can vary according to the type of bond. Some bonds may be intended for only short periods, whereas others may last a lifetime. And the time span of the bond is not decided at the beginning of the relationship but may emerge over time.

Social bonds can demonstrate that those covered by the bond belong together in some respect. But a bond can be made more or less visible to others. For some, a bond may be more acceptable if it is invisible – that only those included know that the bond exists and who belongs to it. For others, it may be important that the bond be visible; for some it may, in fact, be the main reason for being included.

Bonds can be established in several ways: in advance, by gradually emerging, or by agreement. All the bonds into which individuals are born – the bonds to parents, siblings, and clan, and the bonds of citizenship – are determined *in advance*. It is not a question of either party choosing to establish a bond, with the possible exception of the parents who have chosen to adopt a child. These are social bonds that, under certain given conditions, are established automatically with the birth of a child. The bonds are not voluntary, and they are taken for granted. It may be too much to say that they are forced, but basically these bonds do rest on a form of coercion.

Social bonds can also *emerge gradually*. When people meet in different contexts, they eventually get to know each other. They gradually know more about each other, their names, where they live, their phone numbers, and their e-mail addresses, and they start doing things together. This is often how one imagines that friendships or networks emerge.

Social bonds can also be established by *agreement* and by making common decisions about the creation of the bond. It can happen in many contexts, from a job with a company to a marriage. Even a lease or a mortgage for a home can be understood as a social bond.

Expectations and Goals

The vast majority of relationships are formed with a special purpose or focus. The social bonds that bind people to a relationship include communication about how they are expected to contribute, the expectations they have of each other, and what they should do together. It is not merely the purpose and goal that need to be stated, but also how the collaboration is to take place. Should the participants do things together or in different places? How often and where should they meet? The parties in a bond can jointly formulate the expectations, or outsiders can determine them. Expectations can change over time; they are difficult to set once and for all. Even if a bond is designed according to a recognized model, it often needs to be adapted to specific people. On the other hand, it is not certain that the bonds will ever fit perfectly; they will often chafe and feel like obstacles or even shackles. And it may happen that the bonds are broken if people have different or unrealistic expectations of each other.

Transparency

Social bonds are usually long lasting, but even bonds that are expected to last for a short time can be exposed to great stress; they can gradually wear out and the relationship weaken. The participants want to know if their expectations are fulfilled and if they lead to the desired results. One prerequisite for continuing a collaboration is awareness of what the other person has done, because their actions are dependent on each other and may become meaningless if they cannot be adapted to each other. A review of the bond can occur through direct observation, but if many people are involved, they must agree on a way to report and measure how different people meet the expectations placed upon them. It is not only those who are directly covered by the bond who are interested in seeing if it works, however; the checks are often made by others who want the bond to hold firm.

Consequences

In addition to being tested and inspected, bonds must be maintained. And if they are broken, they must be repaired or strengthened. Communication needs to be updated and adapted in accordance with the development of the relationship and the extent to which expectations are met. Communication can be accomplished through feedback or sanctions; those covered need to talk about the design of the bond and give their opinions in the form of complaints or encouragement. And they can hand out sanctions in the form of rewards or punishments.

Communicative Order

The social bonds in a relationship need to be constructed in a way that shows an order of communication – how different types of communication should be mediated between those involved – so that it is clear who is to take the initiative for change or various forms of deliberation.

As a conclusion to this chapter, Table 2.1 shows how a number of established concepts related to the construction of social bonds can be understood when they are connected with what social bonds can do. It is far from a complete account; it is merely a set of examples of what it might look like. In Chapters 3 and 4, I develop an analysis of these concepts and how they can be connected in different types of relationships.

Table 2.1   Forms and contents of social bonds

	DECISION	INSTITUTION	RECIPROCITY
AFFILIATION	employment membership marriage	kinship	friendship
EXPECTATIONS	rules, orders	norms	reciprocation of a similar gift or invitation
	goals	fashion	
TRANSPARENCY	monitoring exams	ceremonies, rituals prejudice	gossip
CONSEQUENCES	promotion	respect	reciprocation of gift or invitation …
	bonus, prize grades exclusion	disrespect/disgust	… or no reciprocation
COMMUNICATIVE ORDER	hierarchy democracy	status	turn-taking

Decisions, institutions, and reciprocity provide different conditions for the establishment of a bond and what belonging means. Employment presupposes a decision by an employer, kinship bonds are primarily institutionally defined and taken for granted, and friendship bonds grow over time.

Different types of communication do not have to be mutually exclusive. Social bonds can be constructed with several types of communication. In a family business, several of the employees may be related to each other. And friends can be employees of the same company. But friendship is rarely established through a decision in the same way as a decision to marry is decided.

Organizations are consistently based on decisions about five organizational elements, but other forms of communication may also occur. Although what happens in organizations is primarily governed by rules or ordering, it does not preclude some of the employees or members being guided by established norms in their way of dealing with each other. Rules and norms may reinforce each other, but if there is a discrepancy between them, it can create tensions in relationships.

In formal organizations, different methods are decided upon to make it possible to observe and measure if and how employees or members fulfil their tasks or what knowledge they have acquired, but traditional ceremonies or rituals can also be used to check the loyalty of members.

Businesses have many ways of rewarding employees who have done well; they can be offered a promotion or given a raise or a financial bonus. Penalties can be in the form of warnings or even a salary deduction. Or the ultimate punishment: exclusion. Grading students can be a form of either positive or negative sanction, depending on the grade. Institutional rewards and punishments can demonstrate respect or contempt. Reciprocating with a gift or an invitation is one way that people can demonstrate that they want a relationship to continue.

Hierarchy and democracy are two schemes for making and communicating decisions that can be applied in different combinations in different types of organizations. Alternatively, the communication can follow a status order or as a turn-taking of initiatives or making invitations.

NOTE

1. In her book, *Governing the Commons: The Evolution of Institutions for Collective Action*, political scientist Elinor Ostrom (1990) explained how a number of so-called common-pool resource projects (CPR) such as mountain grazing and forest CPRs in Switzerland and Japan and irrigation systems in Spain and the Philippine Islands have been made possible. Some of them have been functioning for a thousand years. Her analysis highlighted five so-called 'design principles' that were required to enable successful projects (p. 90): monitoring, graduated sanctions, clearly defined boundaries, collective-choice arrangements, and congruence between appropriation and provision rules and local conditions. In practice, these design principles correspond well with the five functions described here. All these principles were applied in the successful projects; in other, less successful projects, only a few of these principles were applied.

3. Social relationships

Relational sociologists have demonstrated a way of understanding the connection between human actions and social processes – a connection that points beyond the misleading division between the micro and the macro and a view of societies as distinctly autonomous entities. The concept of relationship that has been proposed is insufficient, however; it has yet to be specified and nuanced. We should no longer assume that relationships are only about networks. We need to create a better understanding of the way relationships are created and maintained, and we need to grasp the diversity of social relationships. There are many kinds of relationships other than networks: kinship, friendship, and organizations to name a few.

In this chapter, I emphasize three aspects of the importance of starting this analysis from a foundation of relationships:

1. It is in relationships that people together make society. Through relationships, individual actions are transcended, to be merged into action chains of greater scope.
2. Relationships are surrounded by other relationships, and people are involved in several relationships.
3. Although all relationships are constructed in basically the same way, they differ in terms of their scope, their content, and the bonds with which they are constructed.

First, the study of relationships paves the way for an understanding of the ways in which *people make society together*. When our starting point is relationships, it provides a focus on people's interdependence and how each person's actions are connected with the actions of others in the same relationship – how their actions are propagated, built upon, and accumulated into social processes. Everyone who is included in the same relationship is expected, regardless of internal tensions, to pull in the same direction.

Relationships do not necessarily mean that everyone in the relationship is in direct interaction with everyone else. In relationships that involve many individuals, each person may regularly interact with only a few people and may never interact with others. But their indirect interdependence can be mediated by others.

Second, the image of a relationship also includes a picture of how *relationships relate to other relationships*. One cannot describe a relationship without simultaneously examining its surroundings and other relationships in those surroundings. How the interface with the outside world is constructed, maintained, or changed is an essential part of relationship analysis. We get nothing like that from concepts such as society, structure, or systems. They appear as monolithic totalities with no outside world. Virtually no relationships are self-sufficient or autonomous, but what distinguishes them is that, through their bonds, those included try to differentiate themselves from other relationships by keeping track of who is and is not included, and how they should relate to people and relationships that are not included.

Relationships can be local, but they can also extend across the globe without having to contain many bonds. That a relationship is global in any sense does not mean that it is open, however. Global relationships are often closed yet have many exchanges with the external environment. From within their relationship, the people included try to keep track of these exchanges, whether within families, states, or companies.

Third, there are *significant differences among various types of relationships*: A closed relationship expands through the connecting of several bonds. The number of individuals included in the same relationship varies greatly. As examples of social relationships, Max Weber (1968) mentions states, churches, associations, and marriages (p. 27). There are enormous differences among relationships in this respect: from a few individuals, as in families, to billions, as in Indian and Chinese citizenship.

Knowing the number of individuals involved in a closed relationship is important, of course, if we are to understand how it works and develops. Nevertheless, I consider it reasonable to use the same term to describe relationships that include a small number of people and those including millions. The basic mechanisms and functions of different bonds and how they are constructed are the same, after all, and they connect people's actions to social processes in basically the same way.

In both everyday language and the social sciences, a number of terms are used to speak of closed relationships: families, companies, trade unions, political parties, and gangs. Weber (1968) argued that every type of social relationship is based on a 'meaningful course of social action and a probability of action in some definite way appropriate to this meaning' (p. 27). Different relationships have different institutional foundations. There are notions about the types of actions they refer to, the necessary content for a relationship with a certain designation, and how the bonds are expected to be shaped. Yet each relationship is unique and often deviates in one way or another from the expectations of the outside world.

RELATIONSHIPS AND BONDS

Relationships are clusters of social bonds that are separated from other relationships. Each bond is unique and includes only two parties. When they are connected, interdependence arises between them, even if this dependence is not as strong for everyone. Some individuals may have more options and opportunities than others do. The actions of everyone in the same relationship depend on what the others do and on their previous actions. This situation applies to all types of relationships, whether a family, a gang, a football team, a political party, or a company. If someone messes up, it affects everyone; if someone does a great job, everyone enjoys at least a small part of the success.

Open and Closed Relationships

Weber made a distinction between open and closed relationships. But there are no open bonds; all bonds are tied to unique individuals. Bonds to specific individuals are missing in open relationships. Weber (1968) provided the example of a political meeting, in which everyone interested in participating is welcome. The same would go for a social movement that welcomes everyone who wants to be part of the action. The beginning of a movement is usually not based on membership. In order to be able to start some type of activity, however, there is almost always a small core of people who know each other and form an inner circle in a larger open relationship without bonds. In this way, a movement can involve a large number of people who line up without having to be identified by name. They can show up again and again and be welcome, and they can bring others with them without having to identify them. There may be norms or rules that express how a participant in a meeting, a demonstration, or in some other context should behave, and anyone who violates those rules may be blacklisted and excluded from further activities. It is only when someone is excluded that that person is identified (Grothe-Hammer, 2019; Schoeneborn & Dobusch, 2019).

A movement of this type could serve as an example of a relatively open relationship – one that can be maintained only through the existence of bonds between the people who take responsibility for the relationship. Incidentally, a relationship can continue to exist, at least for some time, without any bonds to other participants. And although Weber noted that there are many variations of openness and closedness, he also saw a tendency for open relationships to turn into closed ones eventually.

Open relationships can be one-sided, in that only one party is interested in observing or trying to interact with the other party. Stalking, espionage, or an agent secretly following a football player that a club is interested in buying would serve as examples of this type of relationship, the major characteristic of which is that it does not include a bond. Such a one-sided, open relationship could be an introduction to a mutual relationship – to a bond – but it can also exist without the other party even knowing about it.

Relationships and Secondary Bonds

A bond is shaped to fit into a particular type of relationship. But individuals who are part of a relationship may have the opportunity to create new bonds, as they adopt new focuses. In this way, individuals who are bonded in one relationship can form another bond in a new relationship or in several new relationships.

In many types of relationships that involve a large number of individuals, there is little interaction among everyone involved. They may not know or recognize each other, even though they are dependent upon each other. But individuals with similar bonds in the same relationship who regularly interact with each other eventually get to know each other. Then their interaction can develop into bonds based on their own norms and values that may differ from the bonds that brought them together. We can call them *secondary bonds*. Siblings in the same family, for example, can develop norms and values that sometimes differ quite strongly from those that their parents advocate, creating their own secondary bonds.

A well-known example of secondary bonds in the sociology of work relates to industrial workers creating norms that differ from those of management about how hard and fast they should work. The classic research in this area was conducted in the 1930s as one of a series of studies in the Hawthorne plant of the Western Electric Company in Chicago. Workers within the group developed norms about what they considered a reasonable effort. They kept track of each other, and those who performed too fast or produced too much were subjected to merciless ridicule and other pressures (Homans, 1951, chapter 3). And there are many other examples in the literature of how industrial workers develop their own collective norms. (See Karlsson et al., 2015.) Secondary bonds such as these can even be developed into formal organizations in the form of trade unions.

In many cases, the people in power in a relationship try to prevent this type of secondary bond from developing by banning contact. Religious communities housing monks or nuns often attempt to counteract the formation of secondary bonds by forbidding personal friendships (Sundberg, 2019). But even in many regular workplaces, there are restrictions on close secondary bonds between employees.

The fact that individuals can simultaneously have several bonds and maintain relationships with others is not a problem merely within a relationship. It can also create problems and ambiguities regarding other relationships in the environment. Parents worry about their children's friends and playmates and try to steer their bonds outside the family in what they consider the best direction. Even for companies or political parties, the bonds of their employees or members outside their own relationship can cause problems if they behave and operate in the wrong context or even have bonds that compete with the companies' or the parties' activities. I explore this issue further in Chapters 4 and 5.

Relationships with Different Types of Bonds

One reason for distinguishing between bonds and relationships is that relationships can be constructed of several types of bonds. Researchers and people in general often mention family bonds, but if one examines their qualities and construction, it is obvious that these bonds are not the same for all family members. A marriage relationship is extended with new bonds when the couple has children, and these bonds have a different character than the original bond between the spouses. A child's bonds are congenital and difficult to dissolve. Social bonds in a family can be expanded with another type of bond if, for example, an au pair is hired to look after the children. Then the relationship can be described as a household relationship, comprising several types of bonds. Or to examine a completely different kind of relationship, the bonds in a gang can also differ; some of them may be based on kinship rather than friendship, which can affect cohesion in the overall relationship.

To understand the dynamics of different types of relationships, an analysis of the bonds that bind people to the relationship is of utmost importance. Bonds play a major role in creating motives and interests and to provide opportunities for influencing the relationship. There are a number of variants of these differences, whether between employees and owners of companies, permanent and temporary employees, members and employees of voluntary associations, or relatives and in-laws.

RELATIONSHIPS AND THEIR COUSINS

There is a wide range of words that can be used to discuss human collaboration. An incomplete list would contain association, bond, circle, clique, company, congregation, corporation, family, friendship, gang, guild, kinship, league, mafia, movement, party, team, troop, and union. The term often refers to the content of a certain type of activity. Congregation, for example, refers not only to people, but to a religious activity; a mafia is probably engaged in criminal activities. But these terms say very little about the ways in which people are involved or the form their involvement takes.

By seeing all these variations of human collaboration as relationships, we have the possibility of examining how they are constructed through social bonds – the conditions under which people participate. We can see if there is a connection between content and form and how variations and changes in form can affect the content.

But there are also a number of more abstract concepts for human collaboration that are not linked in the same way to the content of the activity – such concepts as *collective action, groups,* or *networks*, which can be advantageously understood as relationships and specified through descriptions of how they are constructed through social bonds.

In discussions of collective action, there is often a notion that a collective, if not oppressing individuals, at least limits and diminishes them. The concept of collective action is associated mainly with economic theory. According to orthodox economic theory, collective action in large groups is difficult to explain and appears to be a paradox. How can individuals stand up to participate in collective actions together with many others? When that happens, how are individuals able to get what they want and act in accordance with their particular preferences? But from a sociological perspective, these situations are not particularly strange. As Udehn (1996) noted, the economic theory of collective action 'is apparently falsified by the very existence of society itself. What we see of collective action, cooperation and social order is not what we are led to expect by the economic logic of collective action' (p. 261). Although several attempts to initiate and create collective action may fail, of course, there are so many that succeed and survive that it is not particularly valuable to emphasize the difficulty and strangeness of creating collective action. The question is not how collective action is possible, but how it is formed. If we see collective action or people acting together as relationships, we can see how people complement and reinforce each other's actions. That people act together is normal; individual actions are the exceptions.

An alternative to the concept of relationship could be *figuration*, a word used by sociologist Norbert Elias, who is often seen as one of the forerunners of relational sociology (Tilly, 1998, p. 19). Elias' (1978) model of figuration is not unlike the model of bonds and relationships – seeing people as individuals yet seeing them as society. Figuration stands for how people 'through their basic dispositions and inclinations, are directed towards and linked with each other in the most diverse ways' (p. 15). A figuration, Elias contends, can include a relatively small number of individuals (a teacher and students in a class) or thousands (the inhabitants of a town or city) or millions (the citizens of a nation) of interdependent people (p. 131).

But figuration is more of an analytical concept that can be applied in various contexts, whereas a relationship is ontological and can encompass many existing units of social life comprising a number of bonds. It seems difficult to see a city as a closed relationship, but the notion does work for a state. Figuration is a broader and more abstract concept. Although all relationships can be seen as figurations, not all figurations can be described as relationships.

Before turning to a discussion of an analysis of variations in the construction of relationships, I discuss groups and networks.

Groups

The term *group* is not common in today's sociological texts; perhaps it has been at least partially replaced by *network*. Research on groups is conducted more often in social psychology. These researchers often focus on the way individuals are affected by belonging to a group; they are less interested in the groups as such and what they accomplish or how they develop.

At the beginning of the last century, on the other hand, group was a key concept in sociology. Early in the 20th century, US sociologist George Horton Cooley began to use the term primary groups, which are characterized by a high degree of face-to-face interaction and strong identification – a family or a neighbourhood, for example (Cooley, 1909, p. 23). As a result, larger groups eventually came to be called secondary groups, although the line between small and large groups was not clear. Those who are part of a secondary group do not interact with everyone in the group, and many of the members, Cooley suggests, 'put very little of themselves into it' (p. 252).

Georg Simmel also noted major differences between small and large groups, among which was his emphasis on heterogeneity as a problem for the cohesion of larger groups (Udehn, 1996, p. 282). In the development of sociology during the 20th century, the concept of group came to be reserved for primary groups, and secondary groups have come to be regarded as organizations (Udehn, 1996, p. 288). Organization is a way for large groups to compensate for the lack of homogeneity and direct control (Udehn, 1996, p. 282).

Probably the most well-known theoretical sociological analysis of groups has been made by George Homans (1951), whose goal was to find the common characteristics of the human group. His 1951 book, *The Human Group*, was based on some well-known sociological and anthropological studies of relatively small groups. He analysed the cohesion of groups, using the concepts of activity, interaction, and sentiment. The definition of a group is based on the frequency of interaction; one can distinguish one group from another by measuring the interaction among individuals (p. 84). With this definition, however, the boundary of a group becomes fluid.

In contrast to Homans, Goffman (1961) wanted to make a clear distinction between groups and the more fluid forms of interaction, such as focused interactions or encounters – a distinction that he also applied to smaller groups. Goffman was strongly opposed to encounters being called groups and contended that these concepts are often confused, perhaps because certain rules can be developed, and a division of labour can exist in both encounters and groups. One difference is that an encounter comprises participants, whereas a group has members. A group is perceived by its members to be a social entity, and they identify with the group. A group must also consist of more than two people, Goffman argued, and unlike encounters, a group continues to exist even when its members are not meeting (pp. 7–12). He also noted that social groups could be formally organized (p. 9). In many ways, Goffman's group is most similar to an organization.

The most-noted difference between groups and organizations seems to be that organizations are generally larger than groups and are more impersonal. Yet we know that many organizations are extremely small. The concept of group emphasizes, above all, people located, gathered, or classified together without an explanation for how they are held together and under what conditions.

Instead of seeing groups primarily as collections of individuals, we should examine the ways they are connected through different types of bonds. If we are to discuss groups, we cannot merely ascertain which individuals are involved on any one occasion. We must also consider the conditions under which they are included, how they became involved, and the commitments they have made. In short, what are their bonds to each other and to the group?

Networks

The use of the term *network* is comparatively new in the social sciences. It is only since the beginning of the 1970s that it has become widely known and used. One of those who contributed to the popularization of the term was Mark Granovetter. In a 1973 article, he argued that interpersonal networks could be the most fruitful micro–macro bridge. 'In one way or the other, it is through these networks that small-scale interaction becomes translated into large-scale patterns, and that these, in turn, feed back into small groups' (p. 1360).

Over the past 30 years, networks have been used more and more to describe almost any relationship among people (Thompson, 2003, p. 2; see also Borgatti & Halgin, 2011). A relatively new proposal for a definition was introduced by Borgatti and Halgin (2011):

> A network consists of a set of ties of a specified type (such as friendship) that link them. The ties interconnect through shared end points to form paths that indirectly link nodes that are not directly tied. The pattern of ties in a network yields a particular structure, and nodes occupy positions within this structure. (p. 1169)

In their studies of networks, researchers are interested primarily in the pattern of ties and are less interested in how these ties are constructed and reproduced (Azarian, 2010). They are content with Granovetter's (1973) distinction between strong and weak ties and the importance of the potential strength of weak ties. Differences between strong and weak ties can be understood in terms of the time, emotional intensity, intimacy (mutual confiding), and the reciprocal services that characterize the tie (p. 1361).

Networks are assumed to be non-hierarchical and are maintained through reciprocity, trust, and social capital (Bommes & Tacke, 2005; Borgatti & Foster, 2003; Podolny & Page, 1998). They are established and expanded through people meeting and getting to know each other in various contexts, at school or at work or in an association. They are reproduced because they are embedded in other relationships, and Bommes and Tacke (2005) have therefore likened them to parasites that 'live on the organizations that feed them' (p. 294). Interaction in networks occurs by following such norms as birthday congratulations (Lonkila, 2011, pp. 88–91). Networks can also be based on gossip, but there is no clear decision-making process; people usually just stop meeting with others whom they think are not living up to the norms.

Networks need not have any obvious boundaries; it is the researcher who defines the size of a network (Borgatti & Halgin, 2011). Networks are less static and stable than has been assumed, and their 'ties are constantly being formed, resolved and renegotiated' (Lizardo & Fletcher Pirkey, 2014, p. 36). Networks have no names or identities and do not announce what they are doing. As Bommes and Tacke (2005) suggest, they are silent.

To see all relationships as networks is to miss many key differences in the way networks are established and reproduced. Friendship and kinship differ in significant ways, yet they are both often described as networks. Friendship is the most common example of networking. (See, for example, Borgatti and Halgin's 2011 definition of network earlier in this section.) Kinship is often described as a network as well (Carsten, 2000, p. 25; Tilly, 2005b, p. 45; Young & Willmott, 1962). But seeing both these types of relationships as networks tells us little about the construction of the bonds holding the relationships together. In friendship, the bonds are invisible, and the duration of the bonds is unclear. In kinship, the bonds are lifelong and usually discernible. There are big differences among various networks in what the participants can do together, depending on how their bonds are designed.

As with groups and organizations, the boundaries between networks and organizations are not always clear. With the increasing popularity of networks as a research topic, organization theory soon adopted this convenient concept. The general assumption seems to be that networks have many advantages over other organizational forms: 'many felicitous properties – flexibility, responsiveness, adaptability, extensive cross functional collaboration, rapid and effective decision making, highly committed employees' (Kanter & Eccles, 1992, p. 525). Compared to organizations, networks are often regarded as being 'lighter on their feet' (Powell, 1990, p. 303).

A PLETHORA OF RELATIONSHIPS

Basically, I consider any form of deliberately repeated human interaction as a relationship. We do not have to worry about defining the differences among groups, organizations, or networks. The main thing is that we examine and describe all relationships based on the construction of the social bonds that hold them together and how those bonds can change.

Generalizing the use of the term 'relationship' shows that most of the time people act together and expect their actions to be complemented by the actions of others – that what they do is directed at other people who care about what they do, and their actions, in turn, focus on the previous actions of others. In that sense, collective action is the norm for human beings, and individual action is the exception. Collective action is not strange or paradoxical; nor does it diminish people – on the contrary.

The social bonds that are part of the same relationship can be constructed from different types of communication. In formal organizations, however, bonds consist mainly of decisions. An organization is expected to be constructed of five organizational elements: membership, rules, monitoring, sanctions, and hierarchy. But not all organizational elements necessarily appear together. In other types of relationships, one or a couple of organizational elements can be combined with bonds that are formed in other ways. We can therefore understand some relationships as partially organized, including only one or two organizational elements (Ahrne & Brunsson, 2011, 2019).

Networks are often seen as the opposite of organizations. They are not decided; they emerge gradually through repeated interaction. If we begin to examine many of the relationships that are usually referred to as networks or those in which the people included want to refer to themselves as belonging to a network, we often find that they are partially organized. It is common in many networks – among researchers, for example – to brag about members of the network and to make a list of the members to show others, in order to attract new members. And to be able to meet, members of a network need to appoint someone as convener to be responsible for arranging a workshop or conference. But the bonds will have changed character then; they become visible to others and can be contested. Attention is thereby shifted away from the internal bonds in the network and how those involved can benefit from the bonds, whether by getting a new job or gaining access to social capital. The focus of the now-visible network becomes what the network does – what those involved can achieve by acting together.

There is a connection between what people can do together and how social bonds are constructed. Bonds set limits on what someone can do; different bonds allow certain types of common acts but exclude or complicate others. The construction of the bonds affects the durability and flexibility of relationships. They are also of great importance for the ways in which the relationship is perceived by others in the environment – by those who are involved but not included.

In the rest of this chapter, in order to show how and why different types of relationships are constructed with different combinations of bonds, I examine relationships that are not usually considered formal organizations but may be partially organized. In doing so, I try to find reasons for the use of different organizational elements and their consequences. What connection is there among the content of the relationship, what the relationship is about, and how the bonds are formed? And what happens to the content if the bonds change? Or vice versa: What happens to the bonds if the content changes?

In the next section, I examine four forms of intimacy: friendship, love, kinship, and collective housing, to see how different emotions are related to the form of the bonds. I also discuss the consequences of partial organization for intimate relationships.

In the section that follows, I discuss five types of relationships: collaborative circles, gangs, brotherhoods, mafias, and social movements; provide examples of how relationships can be altered through the introduction of organizational elements; and examine the tensions that may arise in the construction of social bonds.

VARIATIONS IN INTIMATE BONDS

Intimate relationships are characterized by closeness and strong emotions. Those who are part of the relationship know each other well and have a great deal of information about each other – often things they do not want others to know (Luhmann, 1986, p. 158). Intimate relationships do not arise, however, 'as the result of some instinctive process of mutual attractions' (Layder, 2004, p. 66). As in all social relationships, it is relevant to ask how the bonds between those involved are constructed, who are included and on what terms, how to contact each other, and what those involved can expect from each other (Ahrne, 2019).

In emotional terms, intimacy is chiefly associated with love. But love is so multifaceted, Scheff (2006) argues, that it rather 'serves to hide and disguise the nature of human relationships' (p. 112). Therefore Scheff distinguishes among three forms of love – attraction, attunement, and attachment – and there is a clear connection among these types of love and the way social bonds are constructed in intimate relationships.

Love and Friendship

In his 1986 book, *Love as Passion: The Codification of Intimacy*, Niklas Luhmann shows that romantic love is an emotion and a relationship that is binary coded: Someone is either in love or not in love. People asked if they are in love are expected to be able to answer either yes or no (p. 102).

Experience indicates that most long-lasting romantic relationships eventually lead to the formation of a bond based on a decision, and that those who have decided to become a couple convey this information to their immediate environment and expect their friends and relatives to consider them a couple. Romantic love is a relationship that includes only one bond. Many couples go through a series of steps from exclusive dating to living together, often progressing to engagement and marriage. Even though historically there have been many different norms and notions about how a marriage should be formed, each step along the way requires a decision, and marriage bonds have always been shaped at least partly by decisions.

In many countries of the Western world, however, the formation of stable love relationships has changed over the last 50 years (Lewis, 2001). Today, a couple that establishes a long-lasting love relationship does not necessarily get married or even live together, yet they have made a decision to be together. That decision changes their bond to each other and their relationship is seen in a new light by friends and relatives. Government agencies even become involved, determining the legality of their relationship for such issues as child custody and inheritance.

Having declared their love to each other, many people want others to perceive them as a couple, as exemplified, not least, in the discussion of same-sex marriages (Badgett, 2009; Chauncey, 2004; Weeks et al., 2001). Decision making is a process, and the last step in this process of romantic love is significant in order to express the participants' commitment to adhere to their decision (Brunsson, 2007, p. 15). The literature on same-sex marriage provides examples of the significance of turning this decision into a ceremony and expressing that decision in the presence of other people. One woman describes the effect of that ceremony when she married the woman she loves:

> But on the more serious side, I did feel differently afterwards. I don't know what did, I'll try and describe to you. It was like we had, sort of, it was nothing tangible, but it was like something had sort of passed between us that made us belong more really. (Smart, 2007, p. 70)

Friendships have a different character than romantic love relationships. A person can engage in many friendships, and there are different types and degrees of friendship. Friendships are more difficult to define and differentiate from other similar relationships (cf. Luhmann, 1986). But the fact that friendships are more fluid and have a different character than romantic love relationships have does not mean that they are open, and that people can choose to be friends with whomever they want. Like romantic love, friendship is a relationship that can exist with only one bond, but friendship may also sometimes include more than two people and more than one bond. But it is far from certain that the friends of a friend are friends as well.

Friedland et al. (2014) have described the institutional logic of romantic love: 'Love is distinguished first by words; by each telling the other that one is in love with her/him' (p. 354). In friendship relationships, on the other hand, one does not usually talk about the friendship itself or make promises for a lifelong relationship (Alberoni, 2016). Friendships have many similarities to networks. Friends are not considered couples, and their relationship does not have a name.

In the initial phase, there may be similarities between the bonds in a romantic love relationship and a friendship; they emerge and are not decided. But gradually most romantic love relationships develop in a different way than friendships do: They end, or they lead the parties to the decision to become a couple. This is not the case in friendships. That people do not make decisions or agreements about their friendships is confirmed by interview surveys. In response to questions about how people know they are friends, they say that it is a feeling, something that they feel instinctively but not something that can be decided upon (Ahrne, 2014, pp. 77–78).

There seems to be something that renders it impossible to make decisions about friendship; it does not match the essence of friendship. Although many people love their friends, it is a different kind of love than exists in a romantic love relationship. Of the three variants of love that Scheff distinguishes, friendship is primarily about attunement; friends are on the same wavelength and do not have to explain as much to each other as they would to acquaintances or strangers. What is required for a friendship relationship, Thomas (2013) suggests, is wordless understanding: 'that each can count on the other to understand what she or he says in just the way the person meant to say it' (p. 32). Because it is difficult to discuss or make agreements about friendship, research in the area is sparse. Romantic love, on the other hand, gains power and strength from being expressed and explained; furthermore, to become a couple requires a decision that can, in turn, be examined by researchers.

In the absence of a decision, friendship is confirmed by reciprocity. It is by accepting invitations and gifts and by reciprocating with phone calls and other communications that one demonstrates an interest in maintaining the bond. Failure to reciprocate is interpreted as a message that someone is not interested in continuing a friendship. In interviews about friendship, people say that they stop calling or inviting friends who do not phone them or respond in other ways (Ahrne, 2014, p. 136).

Friendships usually do not end through decisions that are communicated. Individuals who do not want to continue a friendship, rarely tell their friend directly – they rarely 'break up' officially. If the bond in a romantic love relationship were to be dissolved, on the other hand, it happens through some form of decision and concerns more than the two people that the bond has included.

The bonds in a romantic love relationship can be formed by decisions in ways other than the decision to become a couple. Norms, preconceived notions about the division of labour in the home, and how the finances are to be managed, largely shape social bonds in traditional marriages, to the extent that a decision is required in order to break with traditional gender norms. In Adeniji's (2008) study on love and marriage, one interviewed woman said: 'Love and relationships must be organized if gender inequality is not to be reproduced in the name of love' (p. 84). In many families today, it is common to have rules for cleaning, cooking, and who should pick up and drop off the children at preschool. The woman quoted here also recounted how she and her partner struggled with a cleaning schedule they had decided upon.

By making decisions about how they want to live together, families have the opportunity to break with traditional institutional expectations and form their own bonds. But it also means that their decisions about how they want to live together can be questioned and criticized by friends, relatives, and neighbours. They may even be brought to the attention of authorities who question the legal rights and impose the legal responsibilities of couples.

Friendships, on the other hand, are maintained with as little decision making as possible. Instead of making new decisions about when to meet, friends often create their own traditions, doing certain things together at specific times – a certain day of the month, perhaps, or once a year. Maintaining a friendship can also be facilitated by traditions such as birthday celebrations, which does not require a joint agreement or even an invitation.

Kinship

Zerubavel (2012) characterizes kinship as a natural bond, sometimes more specifically defined as resting on blood ties (p. 53); it may even be seen to include deceased relatives from previous generations (p. 34). The notion of a kinship career also exists if children become parents and then grandparents. Relationships can span centuries, as individual members die, and new ones are born. In that context, one often speaks of clans or tribes (James, 2006) that usually bear a name – often a common surname – and a clear boundary between those who are included and those who are not (Tilly, 2005b, p. 44).

Returning to Scheff's (2006) three types of love (attraction, attachment, and attunement), kinship would be characterized as an attachment of innate closeness, generating an emotion that may include some people who do not particularly like each other (pp. 112–113). Because the original affiliation never ends, however, kinship remains even without interaction. One could describe kinship as a kind of relational infrastructure; relationships that are available and can be actualized for different purposes that, as Finch (1989) argues, 'you know that you can always fall back on it' (p. 233).

Reciprocity is a key feature of most kinship bonds. But because the affiliation is always a given, it has a character that extends beyond friendship. There are other expectations of when and how gifts, care, or invitations should be reciprocated. It is a kind of deferred reciprocity – an expectation that one will get something back 'in some other time and as yet unspecified place, and possibly from a third party' (Finch, 1989, p. 165).

From a kinship perspective, the bonds to a new-born baby are taken for granted; it is not something that is decided upon, especially if one imagines that kinship bonds begin with a bond between children and their grandparents (Zerubavel, 2012, p. 16). For the child, it is a bond retained throughout life, and one that is crucial to its identity. As Finch contends, 'you are a member and remain so whatever else happens in your life' (1989, p. 234).

Being related incorporates both rights and obligations. Weiner (2013) describes kinships as 'insurance companies into which one is enrolled at birth and from which one cannot unsubscribe' (p. 100). There is a mutual dependence between relatives; they have common resources, a reputation, and a status to safeguard (pp. 34–35), and a need to keep track of each other.

The fact that the biological kinship is often taken for granted can lead to a difference in the assessment of kinship that does not originate from direct descending order. Adoption and marriage are bonds based on decisions, and decisions can always be questioned. In fact, Rothman (2000) has argued that the biological dimension in kinship 'makes us see adoptive parents as not the real parents, aunts and uncles by marriage as not real aunts and uncles, in-laws as not real relatives' (p. 18; see also Finch, 1989, p. 234).

Even if biological bonds are the basis of kinship, they can never represent the whole truth. Relationships that are motivated by blood ties can become far too inclusive over time (Robertson, 1991, p. 43). In practice, therefore, kinship is not limited to natural bonds. Relationships are always at least partly social constructions (Zerubavel, 2012, p. 64), and kinship systems are understood as combinations of biological and social elements (Carsten, 2000, pp. 29–33).

In addition to distinguishing between the biological and the social, we can distinguish between different ways of making social constructions. Broadly speaking, kinship is constructed culturally and institutionally, but how specific kinship relationships are to be counted can also be decided. States are important decision makers when it comes to kinship. In most states, there is legislation that applies to the way kinship is to be calculated, and some states are involved in establishing paternity in connection with inheritance. Rules for how kinship should be counted can also be issued by religious organizations (Weiner, 2013, p. 201).

But relatives can also make their own decisions about their kinship bonds. There is a 'degree of agency in how we identify ourselves genealogically' (Zerubavel, 2012, p. 77). Relatives can together decide how they want to describe their ancestry. By choosing their way of establishing genealogies and describing their genealogical origins, people try to influence their own identity and how other people should perceive them: 'pedigrees and family trees are therefore partly products of the choices we make about which ancestors to remember' (p. 77). New decisions about kinship occur in many contexts: in business dynasties, in royal families, or even when people move away from their families.

When it comes to dimensions of kinship other than membership, everything suggests that there is great variation among different forms of kinship from a historical perspective. In kinship relationships that can lead to special powers – in royal families or nobility, for example – the bonds generally seem to contain much more organization, such as rules and monitoring of various kinds. In such families there are rules about such issues as which titles are to be inherited by which children.

Local clan councils, usually comprising a political and legal assembly of clan elders, serve as an example of kinship involving both hierarchy and sanctions. In India today, for example, it is not uncommon for clan members to demand that such councils settle disputes of various kinds. Because they are not so strictly bound by rules, they can often be more effective than state courts. And the clan may be better able to follow up decisions about such sanctions as exclusion or financial marginalization (Weiner, 2013, p. 12).

But kinship systems are not formal organizations. As Fukuyama (2012) noted, 'The loose, decentralized system of organization is a source of both strength and weakness for tribal societies' (p. 77). For one thing, its leadership is based on status rather than hierarchy. And unless the relatives form a formal kinship association, kinship does not incorporate all the organizational elements; but neither is it a naturally emerging relationship.

Communal Intimacy in Collective Housing

Collective housing is a growing trend in many Western countries. It is sometimes presented as an alternative to traditional families, but the social bonds created through collective housing differ significantly from family relationships. Collective housing units may differ in the size and age composition of its residents, but the bonds created tend to be constructions that bind people together through organizational elements.

Collective housing creates relationships in which people live together and share large parts of their everyday lives, like a shared kitchen. But many of the residents do not know each other before joining the collective; they are selected through the decisions of other residents. Members of a collective are interchangeable, and communal life is organized to handle these shifts in the residential composition. There are rules for joint work in the kitchen and other chores, and often for such issues as guests and the use of alcohol and drugs. In most collective housing units, there are also clear forms, often democratic, for how decisions are to be made.

Although these relationships are not initially based on particularly strong emotional bonds, the residents often experience a sense of closeness and community, such that a housing collective can be characterized by communal intimacy. Rules are not seen as an obstacle to interaction, but rather a prerequisite for imposing a joint direction towards the common goal that can enable spontaneity within a given framework. The social and affective aspects that arise out of joint cooking are usually described as the happy but rather unintended consequences of an obligation that is established to serve primarily functional purposes. The potential for intimacy lies in the situation, in the joint conditions whereby people direct themselves simultaneously towards a shared physical place and a set of joint activities (Törnqvist, 2020).

SOME MORE OR LESS ORGANIZED RELATIONSHIPS

Collaborative Circles

Collaborative circles are examples of how friendships can be developed and changed. They often begin as friendly relationships among some 3 to 8 artists, writers, or other creative professionals of the same age, from the same school, and at the same stage of their careers. Sociologist Michael Farrell (2001) has studied a number of collaborative circles, his most famous examples being the French Impressionists. In most of the relationships he studied, a gatekeeper was central in establishing the circle. It was the gatekeeper who chose who would be involved and who introduced the members to each other. From the beginning, Farrell argues, the members were 'linked only by a common bond to the gatekeeper' (p. 276). In the initial phase of the relationship, one of the members often emerged as a charismatic leader who expressed the vision of the circle.

Farrell distinguished a number of stages in the development of these relationships and changes in the bonds between members. Gradually, they decided on rules for how to meet and cooperate. Eventually, the boundaries between insiders and outsiders became sharper, at which point the relationship was definitely closed. In this phase, the circle was often given a name and an identity.

As Farrell observed, the collective action stage was a turning point in the relationship. It could be about arranging a joint exhibition or publishing a magazine. This stage required more organization and a new type of leader who could represent the circle and negotiate with the outside world. This was the phase, Farrell explained, at which problems and conflict seem to be created, and decision making became difficult (p. 25). And even though some bonds between members remained, this phase was the beginning of the dissolution of the relationship.

Gangs and Brotherhoods

Criminal street gangs provide us with another example of how friendships can change. Klein (2016) has defined a street gang as a sustainable, street-oriented youth group, usually comprising only males, with an identity that includes involvement in illegal activity (p. 16). There is a great deal of variation in the stability of gangs and their construction, but Klein defined as 'durable' a gang that lasts for at least several months. Many new gangs dissolve more quickly than that, and few gangs have a lifespan of more than 10 years. The number of members is rarely greater than 50, and some gangs have an unclear role differentiation and constantly changing membership (Prowse, 2013; Rostami, 2016). Street gangs are sometimes referred to as criminal networks, but they are also seen as expressions of organized crime.

Street gang members are generally recruited from existing friendship circles: childhood and neighbourhood friends, schoolmates, or former cell-mates (Prowse, 2013). In some gangs, kinship can be a way of becoming involved. But membership makes a street gang something beyond a network of friends, acquaintances, and relatives. Even if the recruitment of members occurs among friends, the decision to make someone a member is a change in the social bond to the gang. Through membership, it becomes clear who is involved and who is not, and the boundary between the gang and the outside world is usually rendered visible to everyone within and outside of the gang through some form of attire, insignia, or tattoo.

In street gangs, as in formal criminal organizations such as Hells Angels or Bandidos, members often describe themselves in terms of a brotherhood, which is seen in many contexts as a strengthening of friendship. But there is a crucial difference between the bonds of friendship and the social bonds of brotherhood. Brotherhood presupposes membership and implies solidarity with all other members. Although a persons friends can be friends with each other, this hardly applies to all that individual's friends. Brotherhood, on the other hand, is a relationship 'in which a decision concerning membership determines who is and is not a brother' (Sundberg, 2019, p. 275). Although the members of many street gangs see brotherhood as an ideal, a total solidarity, they have a difficult time living up to this ideal. One reason is their local connection. Members of a street gang have a common cultural and territorial affiliation; the connection with the local community is tight. And because gang members necessarily share their everyday lives with such non-members as friends and relatives, the boundaries of the gang become blurred (Barkman & Palmkvist, 2011, chapter 17). When members have close relationships with non-members, loyalty to the gang is threatened, and the gang's cohesion and solidarity is challenged.

The fact that street gangs are established through friendships is a significant factor in introducing other organizational elements. It seems that it is primarily the members' pre-existing friendship bonds that influence their positions in the gang. Most street gangs fail to make decisions about hierarchy (Decker & Pyrooz, 2015), and much of the decision making rests on the higher status of some members (Ahrne & Rostami, 2019).

In addition to membership, the bonds in some street gangs can be constructed with decided rules, but few street gangs can be described as formal organizations in the style of some of the few large multinational outlaw motorcycle gangs that exist in many countries, and most of which have lasted for more than 50 years (Lauchs et al., 2015).

Mafias

The social bonds that comprise relationships that are usually referred to as mafias are completely unlike networks, because 'relationships within mafias are anything but loose, as evidenced by the fact that it is (almost) impossible to get out (alive)' (Catino, 2019, p. 15). There is a fundamental similarity between different mafias arising from their similar conditions and problems (p. 5). Their establishment has occurred in similar circumstances. (See Chapter 6.) A mafia is hardly a formal organization, but its social bonds include several organizational elements.

Kinship is usually the original basis for membership in a mafia. Recruiting suitable members who can be trusted and who can handle the criminal life is key; a failed recruitment poses great risk. Close relatives are often considered the most loyal members. Because not all relatives have the qualities or abilities required of a mafia member, however, people with the same ethnicity are second best. Becoming a mafia member is a process that can take many years, and most prospective members are subjected to various trials before they can be accepted as members (Catino, 2019, pp. 30–33, 294–296).

Rules are crucial in a mafia, as it cannot rely on laws and regulations in its environment. As Catino (2019) explained, 'They do not live in anarchy; they are subject to the law of the outlaw' (p. 8). But given the risk of disclosure, it is forbidden for these rules to be committed to writing (p. 231). Power in a mafia is personal and based on a person's status and personality (p. 140). Rituals of various kinds are significant elements in the social bonds of a mafia, and social events such as weddings, parties, baptisms, and funerals strengthen the sense of belonging and favour the creation of common values (p. 78).

Social Movements

Social movements are based on the idea of change and are often perceived as ideological experiments aimed at demonstrating the possibility of a community that differs from other relationships. Social movements constitute an order based on equality, solidarity, and voluntariness, on the belief that another, better world is possible (Laamanen et al., 2019). They are often described as the opposite of formal organizations. Rather than members, they have participants; rather than hierarchy, they create consensus; rather than monitoring and control, they are characterized by the desire to create trust and solidarity (den Hond et al., 2015).

Participation in a movement is not based primarily on knowing the others involved, but on a voluntary commitment. Nor is it about any form of reciprocity. Social movements are usually open relationships, at least initially, but the bonds to and participation in the movement are made visible during manifestations or demonstrations. Participants in movements often wear various symbols or signs that indicate their support and participation in the movement.

In practice, however, it turns out that social movements often introduce different organizational elements – rules for the way the participants should behave during a demonstration or manifestation, the slogans they may shout, or perhaps even how they should dress. And given the establishment of rules, it becomes necessary to ensure that they are being followed. Ideally, social movements should be open to anyone who wants to join, but this is not always possible. In certain situations, especially in the case of acute conflict, such as the occupation of a building, people who are judged to be unable to cope with the stress are not welcome. The introduction of organizational elements, a decided order, may encounter opposition from some of the participants who think that these forms of organization go against the very idea of a social movement. One element that is particularly controversial is hierarchy. But without any type of decision-making order, a movement risks a takeover by a small group of participants making decisions that apply to the entire movement (Laamanen et al., 2019). But if, on the other hand, the social bonds that hold the movement together change and are based on too many organizational elements, the movement risks losing the character of a movement and becoming a formal organization. This transformation happens to many movements over time, however, as unwilling as their members may be to admit it.

In the next chapter, I address the five organizational elements of formal organizations: membership, rules, hierarchy, monitoring, and sanctions.

4.   Organizations

In the previous chapter, I outlined a common notion in the literature: groups are small, and organizations are large. But organizations are not necessarily characterized by having many members; there are organizations with few members. Rather, it is the construction of social bonds holding the relationship together that is the crucial determinant of the distinction between groups and organizations. And the bonds in organizations are shaped largely by decisions.

The social bonds are more distinct, more specific, and more detailed in organizations than in most other relationships. They constitute a form of communication that is observable to people other than those most involved, and they leave traces and a lasting impression. Organizations are created not merely through biological or emotional bonds; there must be other agreements involved. The individuals included need not know each other personally or even recognize each other; they do not even need to meet, because their actions can be joined in larger action chains. In an organization, the visibility of social bonds has meant that the organization has a partially independent existence: 'a structure of positions has been created that exists independently of the occupants of these positions' (Coleman, 1990, p. 427).

Although it is not the number of members that distinguishes organizations from other relationships, organizations, by the quality of their bonds, have greater opportunities to include many people. They can also be long lived. Organizations are dominant components in the society around us. Society exists in organizations rather than the other way around. But because organizations are based on decisions, they can fail. Therefore most organizations do not become either large or long lived, and many dissolve after a relatively short time. But those that remain and have been successful become even more significant and can gain great power over people.

To a large extent, human interaction occurs in and around organizations – not only in the form of members, but also as customers, clients, patients, or visitors. There are organizations of different sizes and orientations with different powers and abilities to influence each other. But no organization is theoretically or ontologically superior to any other.

It is not possible to study organizations from either a micro or a macro perspective alone. The social bonds that bind people to organizations simultaneously hold the organization together and form what is usually called organizational structure. And, as Ackroyd (2002) attested, 'Structure is enduring relationships' (p. 74). It is impossible to analyse an organization without addressing the ways in which their bonds affect people's everyday lives: what time they go to work, if they can work from home, if they can take their vacation at any time of the year. The power of organizations over people is exercised by getting them to return to school, to work, or to training, and to get them to do things in certain ways at certain times. But this everyday perspective is inevitably linked to the organization's existence in general: how decisions are made; how the organization develops, perhaps changes or moves; and how the organization operates in an environment of other relationships. From the perspective of a relational theory of organizations, it becomes clear that organizations are not only exposed to the pressures of the environment; they are at least as involved in shaping the world around them.

WHAT IS SPECIAL ABOUT A RELATIONAL ORGANIZATION THEORY?

It is not as strange as one might think that much of the classic theory of organization is about relationships. Organizing is about binding people's actions together, so they intertwine to create something new and larger – something that no one could accomplish alone. Much of classic organizational theory revolves around the functions and qualities of social bonds discussed in Chapter 2. In organizations, we can talk about these functions and qualities as organizational elements. But in traditional organizational theory, the relational perspective is often hidden in a systemic or structural perspective.

Organizations are often described as systems, with a distinction among the images of organizations as rational, natural, or open systems (Scott, 1981; Scott & Davis, 2007). It has been said that organizational theory has evolved from viewing organizations as closed systems to seeing them as open systems. But organizations are primarily closed relationships (cf. Chapter 3). The fact that they are closed does not mean that there are no openings, but that they are monitored and often locked. To be admitted, one must have a key, be recognized, or be able to show proof of permission to enter: an identity card, a membership card, a passport, or a visa. (See Chapter 2; cf. Papakostas, 2012.) Many organizations are open to visitors – customers, audiences, or patients – but the open entrances and exits may also be monitored, and there may be checks for the people who are allowed to come and go. Have they bought a ticket? What time did they arrive? And what did they bring with them on their way out that requires payment? In that sense, organizations are both closed and open. They are closed, because decisions have been made about who can join, and only the members can have a share of the organization's resources. At the same time, organizations are open to transactions of various kinds with other organizations or individuals.

A consistent idea in traditional organizational theory is the contradiction between organization and environment. The environmental perspective was introduced through the so-called contingency theory in the late 1960s. A key point was an emphasis on the notion that there is no best way to design an organization; it depends on the environment in which it operates. The environment can be described in a number of ways. In the beginning, as per Lawrence and Lorsch (1967), variations in the environment were observed as different types of technology. Subsequently, many other environmental factors have been proposed as significant: geography, uncertainty, resource dependence, and culture, for example (Lawrence, 1993; Scott & Davis, 2007, p. 104). But in organization theory, people play a subordinate role in the analysis of environments.

From a relational perspective, one cannot ignore the fact that it is people together that form organizations. More than one person is required to establish an organization, and those people must be willing to commit themselves to deciding upon and performing certain tasks regularly or otherwise supporting the organization's activities. How these bonds are fashioned is crucial for what an organization can do and how it can do things. Through these bonds, an organization is linked to its environment, but this environment need not be a cohesive geographical space.

Organization and Institution

In much social theory, institutions are seen as superior to organizations. Douglas North (1993) argued, for example, that 'Institutions are the rules of the game and organizations are the players' (p. 12). And it is true that institutions are not players; yet organizations can change the rules or ignore them. In Anthony Giddens' (1984) theory of structuration, which has had a certain impact among organizational researchers (see, e.g., Scott & Davis, 2007, p. 25), institutions are more fundamental than organizations are. For Giddens, organizations are first and foremost reflections of institutional practices.

Even in traditional organization theory, the so-called neo-institutional theory has had a strong impact. It was launched over 40 years ago by Meyer and Rowan (1977) with the publication of an article that bore the telling title of 'Institutional organizations: Formal structure as myth and ceremony'. The basic idea behind this theory is that what happens in organizations is primarily affected by institutions existing in the environment. In order to understand what is happening in an organization, one should first look in its environment rather than examining the organization itself. In this way, Brunsson (2020) argues, the neo-institutional theory questions the division between organization and environment (p. 56).

Institutions and organizations condition each other. In an article entitled 'Foundations of the theory of organizations', Philip Selznick (1948), one of the first organizational sociologists in the USA to criticize an overly rational theory of organizations, emphasized the interdependence of institution and organization. Both new and existing organizations, he argued, are always 'subject to the pressure of an institutional environment to which some over-all adjustment must be made' (p. 25).

Institutions matter. They form ideas about how different types of organizations should be designed: what a company or a state should look like and what it should do. There are models for new organizations, whether a shop, a sports association, or a political party. Those who establish an organization have ideas about what it should look like, so that others will know the type of organization it is and what they can expect from it. At the same time, it is likely that the founders want to create something new and unique. They must make many choices and many decisions. Although organizations are unique, it can be favourable for some of them to gain legitimacy by presenting themselves as more like others than they really are. Others may choose to arouse attention and curiosity by presenting themselves as less similar than they are.

From an institutional perspective, Brunsson (2020) argues, organizations are like each other because they are influenced by the same institutions (p. 57). But from a relational perspective, they differ in that they operate in different environments and have different members. Institutions are only part of an organization's environment. All real organizations deviate from institutional notions because of their histories, their environment, and the people they recruit. An institution, on the other hand, has no members and no environment.

Pure Types or Hybrids?

One way to talk about similarities and differences between organizations is to distinguish between different organizational models or pure types. One of the better-known organizational typologies was presented by Henry Mintzberg (1979, 1993) who distinguished among five pure types: the *simple structure, machine bureaucracy, professional bureaucracy, divisionalized form,* and *adhocracy.* He described each type in detail, but in the end, he wondered if any of these types of organizations really exist in a pure form. And his answer, in short, was 'No'. Some organizations may be a pure type, he contended, but most are mixtures, with elements of several types (1979, pp. 468–469; 1993, pp. 284–285).

Bureaucracy, first described by Weber (1968), is a pure type. His bureaucratic model included all five organizational elements (pp. 956–958). But for the most part, it is difficult to determine whether a particular organization, whether government agency or company, could be regarded as a bureaucracy.

Most organizations have some bureaucratic elements such as rules and hierarchy, but even that state of affairs changes over time. Some organizational researchers have claimed that the bureaucratic model has become obsolete. But DiMaggio (2001) concluded in a review of new forms of organization from the end of the 20th century that what has happened is 'an evolution or loosening of bureaucratic structures, not its replacement by something else' (p. 221).

Organizations that do not correspond to any of the pure types are often called hybrids, and they can be described as mixtures of institutional logics (Alexius & Furusten, 2019). They can occur in change processes that are not fully completed, but also arise when an organization tries to fulfil several goals simultaneously (Mintzberg, 1993, p. 290). There is much to suggest that hybrid forms are becoming more common (Czarniawska & Solli, 2016). An increasing prevalence of hybrid organizations points to the importance of highlighting the fact that organizations can comprise several types of social bonds in various combinations.

Instead of asking which organizational model or pure type a particular organization most resembles, one can look at its organizational elements and how they are designed. Then there is no need to think of organizations as hybrids; they can be perceived as having been formed through different combinations of organizational elements.

* * *

In the remainder of this chapter, I first discuss two fundamental differences between organizations and other types of relationships – differences that can be explained by the fact that the social bonds in organizations are constructed through decisions. Membership in an organization is based on a decision – a decision that can be made quickly. No previous contact is needed, whether in the form of friendship, love, or kinship, making organizations more flexible in their recruitment efforts and making everyone in the organization interchangeable. This exchange of members can be facilitated by written rules and developed forms of monitoring and sanctions. Yet, it can still be difficult for many organizations to recruit the members they want, and many fail to do so, but the possibilities exist. The interchangeability of members has had an effect, in that organizations are able to accumulate sizeable resources.

I next discuss each organizational element separately: membership, rules, hierarchy, monitoring, and sanctions. Formal organizations are expected to make decisions on these elements, yet those decisions typically constitute only a small part of all their decisions. In Kemper's (2012) terms, relational activities in organizations can be contrasted to technical activities, which tend to be more common (p. 12).

Instead of starting from different organizational models, I address one organizational element at a time, delving into the way the same elements can be designed in several ways and how bonds in the same organization can have different forms. I discuss why certain organizational elements are sometimes insufficient and which alternatives are applied, providing a more detailed description of social bonds than was dealt with in previous chapters.

REPLACING PEOPLE

For Georg Simmel (1898), the task of sociology was to investigate and explain 'the forms or ways in which human beings exist beside, for, and with each other' (p. 663). He also asked himself how it was possible to explain the superindividual character and independence of such societal forces as organizations. How can we say that it is 'the same state, the same association, the same army, which now exists that existed so and so many decades or centuries ago?' (p. 667). In short, how can an organization survive its members? And the answer is that it can do so by replacing them. The fact that people can and must be replaced, however, does not mean that they are unimportant. As Selznick (1948) stated over 70 years ago, organizations do not function or even exist without people, but no individual can be irreplaceable.

A prerequisite for an organization's survival is that everyone cannot be replaced at the same time. And as Simmel (1898) observed over 13 decades ago, the fact that we can say it is the same organization requires that the change be 'sufficiently slow and gradual' (p. 671). Even though people in organizations are constantly being replaced by new members, the vast majority remain; the new people can, after all, be trained and learn from the others. Again, to quote Simmel:

> By virtue of this fact it comes about that a continuity is maintained which conducts the vast majority of the individuals who live in a given moment into the life of the next moment. The change, the disappearance, and entrance of persons affects in two contiguous moments a number relatively small compared with the number of those who remain constant. (p. 669)

In most organizations, there is an awareness of the importance of replacing people who become ill, quit, or are fired, an issue that necessarily affects the design of the entire organization. Replacements can be made in several ways, depending on the activity, the position, and the availability of potential replacements. In some organizations, it is possible to form bonds that are so clear and specialized that it will be easy to make constant changes. Other organizations prepare for replacements by establishing specific positions for recent hires, apprentices, or trainees, preparing them to pursue a career within the organization. In still other organizations – in political parties or sports clubs, for instance – young people are educated through youth organizations.

But replacing people is far from unproblematic, and many organizations fail, either because no one wants to join them or because they are unable to find suitable candidates. In any case, as Simmel assumed and I discuss in Chapter 6, it may not be obvious that we can talk about the same organization after many replacements have taken place. Is it possible, given organizational change, to step into the same organization twice?

The replacement of individuals in an organization often involves change. And one change that has received special attention in research on such voluntary associations as trade unions and environmental groups is associated with generational change. It has been observed that those who are involved in founding a new voluntary association and have fought for its formation have stronger motivation and that they regard the new organization in a different way than do their successors, who have been, so to speak, born into the organization. This circumstance may apply to free churches, political organizations, and other nonprofit organizations as well (Johansson, 1992, p. 22). For the second generation, the organization's survival may be more important than the goals for which it stands. A similar problem can occur in start-ups when it becomes time to replace the founder (Schein, 1983).

In order for a relationship to develop into an organization with a long lifespan, it must be possible to replace the members. Based on a ranking of 28 popular rock bands, we (Ahrne & Castillo, 2020) examined the interchangeability of their members and noted which bands had turned into organizations. Six of the bands had existed for more than 30 years, with all their members or all but one member replaced several times. Santana was the band with the greatest turnover: 70 members. It is completely dependent on its leader and songwriter, Carlos Santana, who is responsible for the band's survival. He illustrates one of the dilemmas of interchangeability. A strong leader can make other members easily replaceable, but the replacement of a strong leader is always problematic, if not impossible.

There were only three groups that could not continue because they could not replace any of the members, including the first and second most popular bands: the Beatles and Led Zeppelin. In the case of Led Zeppelin, the drummer had a unique style that the others could not or did not want to replace after his death. As for the Beatles, all four members were stars, and their dynamics were too strong for any one of them to be replaced.

People are replaced one by one in organizations, but the personal bonds that can grow spontaneously when people work or perform together without any decisions or instructions create a unique dynamic that can be impossible to supplant. It is perhaps no coincidence that it was the bands that did not last the longest that came out at the top of the list. Something is lost when a relationship is organized.

COLLECTIVE GOODS, GOALS, AND POWER

If people are interchangeable, organizations can become long lived, and over time they can also accumulate considerable resources. One can better understand the importance of interchangeability and collective resources by examining a family. Interchangeability does not exist in a nuclear family. In the event of a divorce, the spouses go their separate ways, the family's property is divided between the spouses, and the original family is dissolved. If one of the spouses remarries, it is no longer the same family. Families are not organizations, although they may be partially organized (cf. Chapter 3).

Even when some individuals leave, the organization's resources remain. The organization remains largely the same, and the collective resources are intact. Simmel (1898) emphasized this notion as one of the prerequisites for the persistence of organizations. An organization, he argued, lives its own life:

> it completely detaches the quotas of possessions from their former owners who contributed them; and it can no more give these back than the organic body can give back to their sources the particles of food that have become part of its substance. (p. 679)

The idea of collective resources is a product of economic theory. Resources can be more or less available to different people. One can distinguish between the degree of publicity of different resources, which relates to the possibility of excluding others from access to these resources (Hechter, 1987, pp. 33–34). Some resources, such as a bicycle, a telephone, or clothing, may be private and owned or controlled by individuals, but other resources – public goods or public resources, like national defence – are available to many people. Most states have a military organization that defends the country in the event of war – a resource from which everyone living in the country benefits, and no one can be excluded. But if we do not limit our analysis to a single state or society, it would be difficult to see military defence as a public good; it is not a resource for everyone in the world, but merely for the people residing in that state. Citizens of other states are excluded. The defence of a country is neither a private nor a public resource; it is a collective resource. From a global perspective, on the other hand, the climate and the world's oceans are public goods.

Individuals cannot normally own or acquire collective resources personally; nor are they available to everyone. Organizations are needed in order to acquire and manage collective resources. The desire to produce and gain access to different types of collective resources motivates people to start organizations or apply to become members. Few people can afford a private golf course. It is a typical collective resource, and most people must create an association in order to acquire and manage it (Hechter, 1987, p. 37). As Hardin (1982) argues, in fact, the vast majority of resources that exist around us are collective resources (pp. 18–19).

We can distinguish four main types of collective resources that are owned and produced by organizations. The three concrete collective resources range from (1) capital; to (2) material resources such as golf courses, buildings, means of transport, machinery, and goods of various kinds; to (3) other members of an organization. In the third case, members perform certain actions together; players in a football club or members of a trade union band together and strike if necessary. (4) Symbolic and intangible resources, such as a well-known company name or an organization's specialized knowledge about certain processes or phenomena are also collective resources, which include such intellectual property as patent rights, trade secrets, and trademarks. Because the intangible nature of intellectual property can present difficulties compared with traditional property like land or goods, most states treat them as a special case and protect them with specific legislation.

Admittedly, everyone who joins an organization obtains a share of its collective resources at some point. It is these collective resources that keep organizations going and create the conditions for activities that provide the work that in turn provides employees with their salaries. Although access to collective resources rarely benefits everyone who participates to the same extent, those who participate do receive a share of the resources, unlike those who do not participate.

As Scott and Davis (2007) have outlined, many definitions of organizations are based on the assumption that organizations have specific goals (pp. 36–37). But several researchers have highlighted the problematic nature of these definitions. Goals are seldom well specified and can change over time. There can also be a big difference between long-term and short-term goals, and an organization can have several goals (Cyert & March, 1992; Perrow, 1986). Instead of looking at an organization's goals, it may make more sense to examine the collective resources an organization has accumulated and the different courses of action these resources provide. The collective resources set the framework for the goals that an organization can achieve.

Possession and control of collective resources are associated with power, and organizations can be understood as power containers (Giddens, 1984, p. 262; cf. Clegg, 1989; Coleman, 1990). Power is relational, which means that it provides the opportunity to make people do things, even if they are resistant because they would rather not do them or because it is against their best interests to do so (Lukes, 1974, p. 27; Weber, 1968, p. 53). Power in this context simply means one's ability to get another person to bend to one's will. Some collective resources, such as various types of weapons, are designed specifically to provide power. But all types of collective resources can provide power in certain situations, to the extent that people are dependent upon them (Emerson, 1962; Etzioni, 1968; Scott & Davis, 2007). For companies, power is primarily a means that can be used to achieve its most important goal: economic profit. For states, power is an end in itself, allowing it to maintain control over its territory.

MEMBERSHIP

People's lives are shaped by the organizations to which they belong, but organizations are also shaped by the people available to it. An organization is not created in a vacuum. It needs to be anchored on the ground, but it can be tightly bound to certain people and places. The construction of these bonds occurs in an interplay and a power struggle between people and organizations. For individuals, it is about who can and may be involved and the terms under which they are involved – what the bond means for their lives. For organizations, it is about the possibility of obtaining people who can and want to perform planned tasks. A perfect match between people and organizations is rare, however.

In organization theory, the term 'membership' is generally applied to all types of organizations (e.g., Luhmann, 2018), but the conditions for membership can vary greatly in duration, motive, and commitment. When looking at the way membership is constructed, fundamental differences emerge among companies, voluntary associations, and states. These differences are crucial for the way they establish, develop, and run their operations. If one wants to go into greater detail about the meaning of affiliation to various types of organizations the concept of membership should be reserved for affiliation to voluntary associations.

Membership is the dominant form of affiliation in associations. In many cases, those who want to be involved can make their own decisions and simply register as members, sometimes by paying a membership fee. Consequently, many voluntary associations are relatively open social relationships. But there are others in which established members reserve the right to decide who should be allowed membership – a protracted process in some cases, with varying types of tests that can extend over several years. Sundberg (2019) discusses monasteries and criminal motorcycle gangs in this context. And in most voluntary associations, members have the right to exclude a member they do not consider to be meeting the organization's requirements and expectations. Voluntary associations are geographically immobile. If there are active members in one place, the organization remains there. Members are not interchangeable in the same way that employees are. Voluntary associations can be spread to other places but are rarely moved.

Most people are born into their *citizenship*, which is the main form of affiliation in states.[1] All states have laws that determine who can be counted as a citizen from birth, often based on combinations of *juris sanguinus* (a new-born baby has the same citizenship as its parents) and *juris solis* (citizenship follows the country in which a child is born) (Heater, 1999). States are obliged to accept as a citizen everyone who is entitled to citizenship according to its laws regarding birth. The social bonds to its citizens renders states tightly tied to a territory.

But states can also obtain new citizens by deciding to award citizenship to people with citizenship in another state, who, for whatever reason, want to change their citizenship or acquire dual citizenship. (For a discussion on dual citizenship, see Chapter 5.) People apply for new citizenship for many reasons: They may be political refugees, they may be following their family to another country, they may want to improve their living conditions, or they may want to acquire a more favourable tax structure. Through the ability to decide on citizenship for those applying, states can choose its citizens to some extent, whether to increase specific professional knowledge, certain language skills, or athletic abilities.

There are two forms of affiliation in companies: *ownership* and *employment*. The formal power in companies belongs to the owners, who can decide who to hire; in which activities they will engage; where their company is to be established; and, if considered appropriate, when and where to move their business to other locations. Employment, by which people are paid to perform a job, is the most common form of affiliation, which varies in length of tenure. But employment is a form of social bond that can be found in other organizations as well, such as states and voluntary associations and in other relationships, such as families.

Of all types of organizations, companies are a form that is characterized in historical comparison by 'unlimited flexibility and capacity for change and adaptation' (Braudel, 1982, p. 433). In many ways, companies represent the typical organization, and most organization theory is primarily about companies. The differences among companies, states, and voluntary associations are given little attention; they are all regarded primarily as organizations.

Employment

In the case of employment relations, it is always the organization that decides who is to be employed and on what terms, but it must ultimately plan its design so that it becomes possible to find suitable people. Over a longer perspective, it is obvious that organizations have been constructed differently, depending on the level of literacy, education, and skills of the people available (Stinchcombe, 1965). The time and space between different demographic processes, such as migration from the countryside to cities and migration between countries is also of great importance for the construction of social bonds in organizations.

The construction of the social bonds between employers and employees is not merely a matter for the two parties directly involved. In most states, employment relations are surrounded by state laws, ranging from age limits and working hours to the rights and obligations of employers and employees. In many countries and in some industries, trade unions are also involved in negotiations concerning conditions for employment.

The same types of production can differ greatly in organizational form due to the availability of labour. But a company can move part of its business to places judged to have a more advantageous labour supply. To see how organizational forms can differ and change depending on the workforce available, we can compare the organization of industrial production in the USA and Japan. A standard theoretical model for industrial organization is Taylorism, also known as scientific management. The name comes from US engineer Frederick Taylor who launched his model in the USA in the early 20th century. As Mintzberg (1979) explained, Taylorism implies that in order to reduce dependence on specific individuals and their skills, tasks are broken down into their smallest components and made as repetitive as possible (p. 74).

The background for the emergence of Taylorism was extensive immigration to the USA during the early part of the 20th century. The extreme division of labour that Taylor advocated proved to be successful in an environment with a steady stream of labour and with the varied backgrounds and language skills of the employees. It mattered little that turnover was large, as it was easy to acquire new employees willing to move into these highly specialized positions requiring next to no training (Littler, 1982). The social bonds were detailed but weak, and they allowed a great deal of interchangeability of employees.

Taylor's scientific management spread through consultants to many countries in Europe during the first half of the 20th century, but in practice the model was applied with great variation and rarely in the extreme form it received in parts of the USA. In many countries, attempts to introduce an increasingly detailed division of labour met with opposition from workers (Ackroyd, 2002; Littler, 1982).

Taylorism in the USA was based on a minimum relationship between the organization and the worker. Conditions differed greatly from those of the USA during Japan's industrialization period in the early 20th century, when Japan was experiencing a severe lack of labour supply and widespread cultural antipathy towards paid employment. To lure people into industry, therefore, employers had to create relatively strong bonds with their employees – bonds that drew heavily on traditional Japanese patterns of relationships and took the form of simulated kinship bonds. A large part of the labour force was young women, and factory dormitories were often established to encourage their longer tenure. Eventually, a corporate paternalism with sick pay, welfare funds, and educational schemes developed. Many large Japanese companies adopted a strategy based on incorporation and utilization of existing social relationships for production purposes (Lincoln & Kalleberg, 1990, p. 22; Littler, 1982, chapter 10). These special circumstances of Japanese industrialization have left their mark on large parts of Japan's current industrial organization.

During the 1980s, the Japanese organizational model gained international attention through the success of its automotive industry. It was based on a model that came to be called *toyotism*, *Toyotaism*, or the Toyota Production System (TPS), because it had been famously adopted during the 1960s by Toyota plants in Japan. Just like Taylorism over a half-century earlier, Toyotaism spread around the world as an exemplary organizational model that provided inspiration for several similar management models, such as total quality management (TQM), lean production system (LPS or Lean), and the just-in-time (JIT) inventory system. The model spread in various ways, as Japanese companies established themselves abroad, and domestic companies around the world tried to apply their variants (Ackroyd et al., 2007a). But, as with the spread of Taylorism, research on various attempts to apply the Japanese model demonstrates that there is no one best way, and that social bonds in working life must always be shaped with a consideration for labour access and national laws and conditions (Elger & Smith, 1994). When organizational models are spread around the world and applied in a new environment, one can talk about a translation. But as Czarniawska and Sevón (2005) have noted, a translation is never the same as the original: 'to set something in a new place is to construct it anew' (p. 8).

Particularly since the latter part of the 20th century, there has been a marked increase in opportunities for industrial companies to choose whatever part of the planet they want to house their production facilities. Through technological development and rationalization (not least through the digitalization of recent decades), companies have been able to become less dependent on both people and places, and companies have been 'freed from conventional temporal and spatial constraints' (Kalleberg, 2011, p. 27). When a company moves, it is a question of parts of its collective resources being moved, while replacing its employees. It is rare for companies to move their entire business to another country, however. More common is so-called offshoring: moving parts of a business and hiring primarily local staff. But with growing digitalization, it is not only low-skilled jobs that are being moved. The decisive factor for whether a job can be relocated is whether it requires direct contact with a specific workplace. Tasks such as programming, accounting, or telemarketing can be most easily handled by outsourced units. Blinder's (2009) calculation shows that as many as one-quarter of all jobs in the USA are currently 'offshorable'.

Rather than moving a company to another country with lower wage levels and perhaps fewer demands from states or unions on how the business should be conducted, some companies have narrowed their organization's boundaries and established relations with companies in another country that can do what the company previously did itself. Such companies create so-called value (supply) chains: organizationally or spatially separated stages of an entire production chain (Gereffi & Fernandez-Stark, 2011).

The fact that some companies – construction companies or service companies, for example – are more location-dependent for their operations than others are does not necessarily mean that they are completely dependent on their immediate environment for recruiting labour. Even for site-specific and site-dependent organizations, the environment has been globalized, or at least expanded through various forms of transnational subcontracting. Construction companies in Germany, for example, can hire workers employed by a subcontractor in Poland. In Germany, the organization of work on many construction sites is adapted to a division of the workforce into three layers, with different bonds to the employer, depending on the nationality of the employees and by whom they are employed – whether they are employed by domestic companies, are transnationally posted workers, or are workers without permits who are in the country illegally (Lillie et al., 2014).

It has become increasingly common to hire labour from employment intermediaries. In the USA, it is estimated that more than half of the nation's companies take advantage of this opportunity, particularly in hiring for peripheral tasks. For their core businesses, on the other hand, they are keen to maintain internal continuity in competence and loyalty. There may be problems with work management if permanent employees work with employees hired through intermediaries, who are likely to have weaker bonds to the company (Kalleberg & Marsden, 2005).

Employees and Members of Voluntary Associations

Members' bonds to voluntary associations are rarely as detailed or extensive as are the bonds between employees and their employers. Although there is a great deal of variation among voluntary associations in how closely their members are connected to an activity, members of voluntary associations, unlike employees, can often decide in which activities they want to participate. Yet, there are specific tasks that must be performed, whether assignments on boards, in administration, or in more practical field work. If some members hold these positions for a long time, there may be a clear stratification among members, which can create problems for internal democracy – an issue

I discuss later in this chapter. There are also divided opinions about how good it is to hire people to perform such tasks. It is sometimes claimed that the association's values and the whole idea of a voluntary activity are threatened if the association has paid employees. In his book on political parties from the beginning of the 20th century, however, Robert Michels (1962) argued that employment can provide people with the opportunity to devote themselves fully to their membership, if they are not in a financial position to participate on a volunteer basis. Thus, employment of such members, he argued, would mean that voluntary associations would not be dependent primarily on people who could afford to engage in unpaid volunteer work (pp. 135–140).

But differences in the social bonds between volunteers and employees can have repercussions when members and employees work together on roughly the same tasks. Contradictions can arise regarding expectations of what to do and how to relate to their common tasks. Volunteers tend to have a more idealistic approach to people to whom the work is directed, whereas employees tend to become more distant and professional. Members may make excessive demands on employees to show stronger commitment and to show up at odd hours. In a growing professionalized voluntary association, however, the members' influence may be threatened, and their efforts may be limited to serving coffee, while the employees take care of contacts with those to whom the organization is directed (Chartrand, 2004).

Many new voluntary associations do not seem to be as dependent on their members as the older, more established voluntary associations are, either for their activities or for financial resources. There is a rationalization of many voluntary associations when employees are increasingly performing the activities – when the business becomes professionalized (Papakostas, 2012, p. 157). Organizations are developing faster than was once the case, and sponsorship from companies or states may provide them with more money than they can obtain through membership fees, allowing them to hire people rather than relying exclusively or even heavily on volunteers. These volunteer members are then referred to as 'support members' and are subject to losing influence.

The decreasing importance of membership in voluntary associations finds other expressions. People can contribute to a voluntary association without becoming members by engaging in contributorship. In this way, voluntary associations become more like open relationships. An organization may be able to find more participants if they do not require them to become members who fully embrace the organization's values. But even non-members must follow the rules of the organization (Grothe-Hammer, 2019).

RULES

The expectations of an organization are expressed through rules: What should everyone do, and how and when should they do it? Rules are a way of governing and holding an organization together, thereby enabling collaboration among many people without their having to meet or see each other. Rules make it possible to control from a distance in both time and space (Ahrne & Brunsson, 2004). There are also rules for employees' or members' contacts with customers, clients, or patients, in order to provide them with equal treatment.

Together, rules form a large part of what is usually referred to as the organization's structure or, as March et al. (2000) suggested, as 'carriers of organizational knowledge' (p. 186). A set of rules is an expression of an organization's collective experiences and constitute part of its organizational memory (Perrow, 1986, p. 26).

Rules are formulated and set through decisions. Deciding on rules can be a way of breaking with or replacing norms for how people in the organization should behave – how they should dress, for example, or even, as in the military, how they should greet each other. But most rules do not replace norms; they state how, where, when, in what order, and by whom things should be done in order that they flow in the right order. Such rules are imposed in order to avoid delays; cheating; duplication of work; and not least to facilitate the interchangeability of people, thereby allowing more people to perform the same tasks and to replace each other when they are ill or leave the organization.

Rules can be changed through new decisions, and they are often (but not always) easier to change than norms are (cf. Chapter 2). One can understand rule changes in a dynamic that includes action, history, and rules. As March et al. (2000) suggested, 'actions are translated into history, history is translated into rules, and rules are translated into actions' (p. 22). New experiences provide a basis for new rules.

It is difficult to imagine an organization existing without some rules. It would have to be a new and extremely small organization with people who know each other well, where new decisions are made for each new activity, or where someone who leads the work distributes orders on an ad hoc basis directly to subordinates. Although there is great variation in the number of rules on which an organization operates, rules are one of the most distinctive features in Weber's (1968) description of bureaucracy (p. 956). In an organization characterized as a bureaucracy, activities are built around rule following and rule interpreting. In some organizations, the activities are completely dependent on rules – in organizations (and they can be authorities or companies) that deal with insurance, for example. Such organizations are usually seen as typical bureaucracies. But there are other organized activities, like organized sports, not usually described as bureaucracies, that are constructed almost entirely through rules.

There are several factors that reduce the need for rules – installing advanced machines that perform some of the work steps, for instance. As Perrow (1986) suggested, 'The rules are built into the machine itself, and the organization pays for those rules when it buys the machine' (p. 22). These words, written 35 years ago, have become even more relevant in the 2000s with the ever-increasing computerization of businesses. Now one can also speak of what Kirchner and Schüßler (2019) refer to as an 'algorithmic bureaucracy'.

In his typology of organizations, Mintzberg (1979) distinguished between what he calls a machine bureaucracy and a professional bureaucracy. But again, it would be difficult to determine where the boundaries would be set between these two types of organization; rather, their differentiation must be understood as tendencies. In an organization with many professional groups, such as physicians or researchers, there is less need for rules, because professionals bring their own rules into the organization (Perrow, 1986, p. 23). In many organizations, conflicts can arise when professional groups oppose management decisions that go against professional rules and values (Sarfatti-Larsson, 1979). There is much to suggest that such contradictions have become more common with the introduction of new governance methods in the wake of New Public Management (Ackroyd et al., 2007b; Hjort, 2007).

Criticism of Rules

As March et al. (2000) famously stated, 'No one likes rules, yet everyone insists on them' (p. 192). Or to quote Perrrow (1986), 'We would all prefer to be free of them' (p. 24). When something goes wrong in an organization, the rules are often blamed – rules that are called stupid, unnecessary, rigid, unfair, or unclear and incomprehensible. Once rules become institutionalized, knowledge about their origins and reasons for their existence are often minimal (cf. Selznick, 1948), and they are taken for granted. Even if rules are documented, they may never be read by most members of the organization. But as Perrow (1986) noted, 'good rules are often those that are rarely noticed' (p. 25) – rules that people do not even realize that they are following. People generally learn rules from each other, have poor knowledge of how they are connected, and may simply ignore them. It is mainly rules that cause problems that people notice and complain about – not the rules they follow mindlessly.

Rules have a tendency to multiply. Rules can easily beget rules. Although there is little research on this issue, James March and his colleagues (2000) at Stanford University found that the accumulation of rules occurs at a decreasing rate, and that the growth of rules was due to the emergence of new problems.

An increase in rules could be interpreted as evidence that individuals in the organization have become wiser, but the reality may not be that positive. There is a lag and a path dependence on how the rule system develops. It reflects not only the current reality of the organization, but also an inefficient history, incorporating a collection of residues of past histories (March et al., 2000, pp. 193–196). Rules have limitations; when based on the organization's previous experiences, they do not always reflect the organization's current reality.

Inadequacy of Rules

There is a tendency in all organizations for members to shield themselves from their surroundings, at least partially because of the specialization of positions pulling in different directions and a need to coordinate activities. For specialists with direct contact with the environment, it can be difficult to spread their knowledge within the organization. They must often use forms and codes to report various activities and events. It is easier to report sales figures or viewer figures than it is to account for customers' or viewers' attitudes towards specific parts of a business. As March and Simon (1958) mentioned over 60 years ago, 'It is extremely difficult to communicate about intangible and non-standardized objects' (p. 164). Internal communication often hides uncertainty about what the environment really looks like. As March and Simon noted, 'The particular categories and schemes of classification it employs are reified, and become, for members of the organization, attributes of the world rather than mere conventions' (p. 165).

The risk of being shielded from one's surroundings becomes particularly obvious and has greater consequences for an organization in an environment undergoing rapid change. As Mintzberg (1979) noted, rule-governed organizations have seen everything before (p. 325). But in an environment in which many new phenomena are emerging, an organization must find other ways to function.

Sociologists Burns and Stalker (1961) discovered a new phenomenon in their classic survey of late-1950s Scottish industrial companies, published in their book, *Management of Innovation.* Many of the companies they studied were of the traditional type, with highly specialized tasks and detailed rules for the execution of work. But others had a continuous redefinition of the content of various tasks, and decision making was decentralized. The explanation for the differences was found in the organizations' environments. The traditional form, which they called *mechanical*, was typical of companies in a stable environment with a secure market for the company's products. The decentralized form, which they labelled *organic*, was typical of companies that did well in an environment with major changes. In a highly changing environment, it is difficult for an organization to design positions in detail using rules or standardization, as they can quickly become obsolete and inadequate. Thus, organizations operating in a rapidly changing environment must rely more on employees' assessments and knowledge to adapt their operations to new conditions. This approach can create problems in shaping social bonds, however. When bonds are loose, the organization becomes more dependent on the person holding the position. In this type of organization, an individual's commitment and identification with the organization's goals become increasingly important.

The term 'organic' is reminiscent of a living being; it suggests something that has emerged naturally rather than being constructed and comprising parts that do not really seem to fit together. In an organically grown product, there are no gaps or joints or even any bonds. Burns and Stalker's organic organization has since been relabelled in the literature (cf. Marshall, 1990, p. 99). Mintzberg (1979) used the term *adhocracies*, but they have also been called *flat organizations*, *postmodern organizations*, or even *networks*. They are often, but not necessarily, relatively small, and often include services, information, or research (Ackroyd, 2002; Heydebrand, 1989). This organizational model is often described in positive terms and represents the dream of the zipless organization – one in which everyone knows what to do and how to do it, and everyone pulls in the same direction.

Schein (1983) contended that such organizations have developed a strong culture: 'Organizational culture, then, is the pattern of basic assumptions that a given group has invented, discovered or developed in learning to cope with its problems of external adaptation and internal integration' (p. 14). Although organizational cultures can usually rely on norms rather than rules, Alvesson (2015) argues that 'even a strong organizational culture can be problematic in a changing environment. It locks in thinking and does not change with the environment; rather the opposite' (p. 89). A strong organizational culture also reduces the substitutability of employees, making it difficult for new employees to fit in.

In organizations that operate in a changing environment, the flow of information is heavy, and communication is extremely time-consuming. As Mintzberg (1979) stated, 'people talk a lot in these structures' (p. 463). Coordination in an adhocracy requires many meetings and conferences. Mintzberg also noted that adhocracies are unstable, just like the environment in which they operate. It is difficult to keep this form of organization together for long, and there is a tendency for the social bonds in adhocracies to change over time in one of two ways: towards the introduction of more rules and a clearer hierarchy or towards dissolution (p. 456). This change can take place in different ways and at different rates in different parts of the same organization. The need for rules can vary depending on activities and conditions in the environment, and different parts of the same organization can operate in different environments. Basically, this dilemma is about how an organization should tackle what

Thompson (1967) identified as the administrative paradox: the simultaneous search for security and flexibility (p. 150).

In today's world of operations in a global or almost-global environment, it is likely that more and more companies and other organizations will have to adapt to faster-changing environments that make full-scale rule management difficult. Employees need to interact with each other more than they did previously, which may explain the increasing number of meetings that have been observed in most organizations, despite the digitalization of many businesses that could have been expected to reduce the need for people to interact face-to-face. Meetings can fulfil valuable functions for holding together and navigating an organization in a changing world. They provide opportunities for necessary discussions and exchanges of information and experiences, and they can make things happen (Sandler & Thedvall, 2017).

Meetings of members or employees of an organization can occur in various contexts, but they are usually predetermined gatherings, often organized in a recurring chain, in special rooms for a small number of people, usually by invitation (Hall et al., 2019, p. 57) and under specific rules for the way they should be conducted. A meeting is considered beyond a spontaneous conversation in a corridor or a lunchroom. Like rules, meetings are the subject of much criticism and dissatisfaction, usually focused on their inefficiency and lack of necessity.

HIERARCHY

In a relationship involving many people, it is ideal that the participants have a common idea of how initiatives should be taken in order for things to be accomplished. Hierarchy is a basic element in Weber's (1968) theory of bureaucracy (p. 957). But hierarchies exist not only in bureaucracies; they are necessary elements in all organizations.

The term 'hierarchy' is sometimes used as a synonym for organization – one may speak of market and hierarchy or market and organization (e.g., Williamson, 1975). This wording suggests that hierarchy would be the most basic feature of an organization, perhaps because people making decisions on behalf of others are characteristic of any organization (cf. Chapter 2). But the fact that organization is based on decisions does not make hierarchy more important than other organizational elements. And hierarchy should not be confused with such other elements as monitoring (Rajan & Wulf, 2006).

A hierarchy is a decided order for making decisions. Based on one's position in a hierarchy, that person knows what to do, when and how to do it, and in what order. Hierarchy allows members to take advantage of the organization's opportunities for coordination and ensures that business flows in the best way possible, given the conditions available.

The importance of hierarchy is exemplified by a position, the incumbent of which has an overview of the entire organization and can distribute efforts and tasks, like the conductor of a symphony orchestra. If an orchestra were to play without a conductor, some instruments could dominate, and the brass and percussion could be heard over the violins and the harp (Abrahamsson, 2007, p. 90).

Hierarchies are often described as vertical – as extending from top to bottom. Organizations are sometimes likened to pyramids, with their small top and wide bottom. The pyramid is also a picture of a hierarchy, which tapers towards the top, where one finds the person with the real power. But it is a picture that seldom matches reality because hierarchies come in many different shapes. In many states with a democratic constitution, decision-making power is ultimately derived from the citizens through elections; and in most voluntary associations, it derives from their members. In such organizations, the decision-making process is not pyramid-shaped, and barely even vertical, making it pointless to discuss whether relationships are horizontal or vertical (cf. Luhmann, 2018, p. 257). When the owners are included in an overview of the decision-making process in a company, a pyramid does not necessarily appear either, and the picture can be quite complex. Because the concept of hierarchy is drawn with such associations, it may be more appropriate to use the term 'constitution'. But because hierarchy is an established concept in organizational theory and constitution is primarily a political science concept, I prefer the term 'hierarchy' to refer to the organizational element that denotes a decision-making process.

Hierarchy has to do with power; it is a decision-making order with the goal of turning decisions into action, to make something happen. What characterizes power in a hierarchical position is its legitimacy (Pfeffer, 1981). It is appropriate, therefore, to distinguish between power and authority, with authority implying that the organization's members or employees have agreed in principle to adhere to the decisions made. As Barnard (1968) defined it, authority applies to acts that are to take place on behalf of the organization and that are to be within the members' or employees' zones of indifference (p. 169). Authority, then, is built into the position and is 'to a considerable extent independent of the personal ability of the incumbent of the position' (p. 173). Barnard contrasts authority with leadership, which depends on personal qualities, power resources, or status. But people are interchangeable in hierarchical positions, and authority should not depend on personal characteristics.

A legitimate decision-making order makes power visible; it allows those affected by decisions about such other organizational elements as rules, membership, monitoring, or sanctions, to know who made the decision, giving them the opportunity to appeal, protest, or simply ask questions. Without hierarchy, it becomes uncertain who decides and who is in charge (Perrow, 1986, p. 26).

Without a decision-making order, strong leaders or people with contacts or special resources can have more space and opportunities for dominance without assuming responsibility. The lack of hierarchy or constitution can lead not to freedom and spontaneity, but to what Jo Freeman (1972) referred to in the title of her much-discussed article, 'The tyranny of structurelessness'.

Hierarchies can be formed in many ways, and people can have legitimate reasons for discussing how a hierarchy should be formed and who should decide what. If people are critical of the hierarchy, they can suggest change or fight for change. But if they want the organization to remain intact, it is foolish to suggest that the hierarchy (or constitution) should be abolished altogether.

Authority Versus Power

> Organizations are hard to run; people don't always do what they are supposed to do. They also reflect diverse, conflicting external interests, and diverse, conflicting internal interests. Information and knowledge is always insufficient, and the environment is often hostile and always somewhat unpredictable. (Perrow, 2007, p. 292)

Decisions made for others about what they should do and how and when they should do it are attempts at getting things done, but it is never certain that those decisions will succeed. The authority and legitimacy behind a decision may not be self-evident, strong enough, or well enough substantiated. The strength of authority is an expression of people's dependence on the organization, of the necessity for them to keep their jobs or their membership, and of their dependence on the survival of the organization. Against all of this can be set opportunities for individuals to ignore a decision, to do things in the way they consider best, or to do nothing at all. Their dependence on the organization is then set against the organization's dependence on them. Individuals or groups can control resources that provide power in many situations. Mechanic's (1962) classic article, 'Sources of power of lower participants in complex organizations' emphasizes that the possession of special information that is crucial in certain situations or control over and knowledge of machines or other equipment can give power to the person who possesses these resources.

Crozier (1964) conducted a classic study in the organization literature about a group of machine repairers in a tobacco factory who possessed unique knowledge about repairing broken machines. Because all the factory's operations were down when the machines did not work, which happened frequently, the entire factory became dependent on their efforts. As a result, these repairers were able to make far-reaching demands regarding their working conditions and wages. Pfeffer (1981) later addressed this case, suggesting that the repairers' knowledge had not been sufficiently documented, rendering them irreplaceable (p. 113).

In many bonds within an organization, hierarchical authority can be questioned, given the conflict of interest or a lack of agreement on how certain things should be done. Such potential conflict can arise between shareholders and a company's management. The owners have the legal authority to make decisions, but because managers, unlike the owners, have actual day-to-day control of what happens in the organization, they can enjoy considerable independence and opportunities to make decisions with which the owners do not agree – a situation that can be difficult for the owners to discover and remedy (Ackroyd, 2002, p. 102).

A similar problem exists in many voluntary organizations, which Robert Michels (1962) described as the 'iron law of the oligarchy' in his book on political parties first published over a century ago. Michels highlighted the difficulties for party members in gaining a decisive influence over the practical activities of parties. Those who exercise the day-to-day leadership of a party inevitably receive more information and gain greater knowledge about the political situation and how it can be handled in practice than do the other members. In addition, it is necessary in sharp political situations for those in authority to make decisions quickly, which overrides the legitimate decision-making system and can rob members of their access to democratic procedures (p. 70). The same problem can exist in relationships between politicians and civil servants in state administrations.

Hierarchical Variations

Hierarchical variations can be described with the term *span of control* – the number of subordinates for whom a boss is the direct supervisor. A company president with 2 vice-presidents, then, would have a span of control of 2, whereas a symphony conductor may have a span of control of 100. Another aspect of hierarchy is its depth, which is inversely related to breadth of the span of control; it is often said, therefore, that it is necessary to reduce the number of decision levels in an organization in order to increase the span of control. Perrow (1986) conducted a review of empirical studies of the 1950s and 1960s on the relationship between the breadth and depth of organizational hierarchies. He concluded that it is not at all certain that a reduction in the number of decision levels is the same as a decentralization and spread of decision-making power in an organization. It all depends on the nature of the activity (pp. 30–33).

In their survey of large US companies of the 1990s, Rajan and Wulf (2006) demonstrated that the depth of hierarchies has decreased by almost a quarter, even as the span of control has increased. This change can be understood as a centralization of businesses, in that CEOs have more contacts further down the organizational hierarchy. But various decision-making functions have also been delegated to lower levels, the authors argued, a development explained primarily by the need for faster decisions due to a rapidly changing environment with increased global competition.

Research on span of control and depth of hierarchies nevertheless provides a limited picture of decision-making chains in organizations. If we include owners in a company's decision-making chains, things become more complicated. And when we examine the hierarchies of states, the relationship is among voters, politicians, and civil servants. There is room for many variations here.

MONITORING

In a temporary interaction, everyone involved can observe what the others are doing and adapt their actions to what they see happening around them, but it is not as easy in a relationship in which people are doing things in different places. Rather, the bonds between those who are part of the relationship must include common ways of conveying information about their actions. In order to achieve coordination, one hand must know what the other hand is doing. That is what monitoring is about, and it can be accomplished in various ways.

The goal of those who organize is to coordinate the actions of what is often a large number of people in such a way that they complement and reinforce each other: 'to make their efforts fit together' (Perrow, 1986, p. 128). This need for monitoring is not primarily about a suspicion that employees, members, and citizens are trying to dodge their responsibilities, but about communicating what they have done so others can assume the same tasks. The term 'monitoring' is also referred to as 'documentation' in the organizational literature. Documentation was a key element in Weber's (1968) bureaucratic model (p. 957), which emphasized the importance of written documents – the files – which are needed so others can learn what an employee has done in a particular case. But written documents can have a different design, even if the purpose is basically the same. A great deal of documentation is currently done digitally, and often through photos that show the work that has been done. And documentation can extend far beyond what we usually refer to as bureaucracy. The form taped to a wall of a toilet cubicle at an airport on which the cleaner notes when the toilet was last cleaned is documentation as well.

Routines for documentation are a prominent feature in the historical development of contemporary organizations. A text entitled 'The origins of organizing in the sixteenth century' indicated that guidelines for letter writing and sending letters were significant elements in such organizations as the Catholic Jesuit order. Letters were not a private matter but were to be distributed according to certain routines. Letter writing was a way of conveying over long distances information about completed tasks, and they could serve as sources of increased knowledge and awareness of individuals (Bento da Silva & Iordanou, 2018).

Although it is reasonable to think of monitoring primarily as a way of transmitting and conveying information in a relationship in order to enable or streamline the coordination of efforts, monitoring also fulfils other functions. Depending on the organization's purpose, various things can be monitored and controlled – the presence of individuals at a meeting, exactly what they did or did not do, how much they have accomplished, what they have learned, or the quality of what has been done. And it is not merely individuals who are observed and controlled; it can be working groups, entire departments, or special units. Supervisors also need to be monitored.

How Does Monitoring Work?

Because organization involves the coordination of people's actions, opportunities for monitoring and learning and keeping track of what others are doing permeates the entire construction of an organization. Surveillance exists because it provides an objective substitute for personal opinions, feelings of like or dislike, gossip, and rumours.

Monitoring can be done by increasing visibility, and the decision to use specific architectural designs in areas where people work or meet is one way of accomplishing that end (Hechter, 1987; Papakostas, 2012). As Perrow (1986) emphasizes, monitoring is not noticeable in a suitably designed environment; rather, design can serve as an unobtrusive control, allowing those who work in the same premises to see what the others are doing (p. 129).

Michel Foucault (1979) described an opposite architectural model in his book, *Discipline and Punish*. This monitoring model, called Panopticon, can be designed so that the individuals who are observed cannot see each other or the person who monitors them. It treats the individual as 'an object of information, never a subject in communication' (p. 200). This form of surveillance originated in prisons, but it can also be applied to the monitoring of workers, making 'it possible to note the aptitudes of each worker, compare the time he takes to perform a task' (p. 203).

Arranging regular meetings or similar events is another way of creating visibility. Meetings can have many purposes, such as the exchange of information and planning, but as Schwartzman (1989, p. 239) argued, they can also be used for monitoring, to keep track of attendance, for instance, to see who was interested and committed enough to turn up at a meeting, and to observe their participation.

Meetings can have ritual elements 'that require members to perform certain acts in public' (Hechter, 1987, p. 151). Public examinations in schools and universities are examples of such ritual visibility, as are oral presentations of

academic dissertations (Papakostas, 2012), annual meetings of voluntary associations, or general meetings at which those responsible for the business must
report what they have achieved, and members or shareholders can ask questions – at least in principle. The concept of monitoring may have a negative
connotation, but not everyone dislikes being observed. In Sundberg's (2015)
study of the Foreign Legion, Legionnaires reported that they wanted their
superiors to see them, because 'then we are not there for nothing' (p. 158).

The technology used in production – a conveyor belt, for example – can also
be designed for monitoring (Edwards, 1979). When the bonds to an organization are linked via machines or technology, the technology serves a controlling
function. As Marglin (1974) argued, the original construction of factories in
the early days of industrialization was not so much to increase production
capacity and efficiency as to create opportunities for monitoring workers, to
ensure that they worked harder and longer.

> The key to the success of the factory, as well as the motive behind it, was the sub-
> stitution of capitalists' for workers' control of the production process: discipline
> and supervision could and did reduce costs without being technologically superior.
> (p. 84)

In the 21st century, technological development through digitalization in
various forms offers the best opportunities for monitoring employees – not
only in the manufacturing industry, but perhaps above all, in the services
industry. Thus, telephone conversations are recorded and meetings with customers are filmed (Hall, 2010). Digitalization has created new opportunities
for monitoring that can dominate an entire workplace in such areas as call
centres. When technology controls work, monitoring becomes an obvious
part of the work process rather than a task performed by special supervisors
(Callaghan & Thompson, 2001).

Yet, there are large parts of an organization's activities that cannot be made
visible to others. One way of monitoring activities that are difficult to observe
is to turn to those that the organization is targeting as customers, students, or
patients, usually via the Internet. Students are asked to evaluate their teachers,
and customers are asked to evaluate the service they have received. This form
of monitoring, however, runs the risk of collecting personal likes, dislikes,
gossip, and rumours.

The opportunities to create visibility differ significantly over organizations,
activities, and various parts of the organization. At one end of the continuum
are spies, whose visibility is extremely limited, although they are often secretly
monitored. At the other end, the visibility of professional sports figures is
virtually total. It is difficult to imagine any group so completely overseen by

referees, coaches, players' agents, and audiences as are the players on professional teams.

But there are also tasks for which the results tend not to be visible, either to others within the organization or to those directly affected, such as students, clients, or patients – tasks that require planning or investigation, tasks that require a long time to complete, and tasks performed by specialists that are difficult for outsiders to assess. Activities under the auspices of the state, in which results are often unclear – activities in such areas as preventive health care, crime prevention, elder care, and psychiatric care – can be difficult to monitor and control.

The increase in this type of task has led to new forms of monitoring, different methods of evaluation, and the development of standardized quality measures to enable monitors to compare activities. New Public Management (NPM) is the common umbrella term for many of the new attempts to control and monitor activities (Christensen & Lægreid, 2001). NPM consists of relatively diverse types of methods of control that aim to increase efficiency and reduce costs. NPM has been developed in various places and spread to many countries, not least through the OECD and the EU.

But, as with all monitoring, there is a significant risk that the methods will have an unintended controlling effect on the activity itself. Critics of these new forms of monitoring, such as Power (1997), have noted that 'values and practices that make auditing possible penetrate deep into the core of organizational operations' (p. 97). There is a risk that tasks can be organized – first of all, to give positive evaluations and to create quality measures that appear to be highly valid. Standardized quality measures in health care can be based on measures that govern how care staff organize their work, for example, without regard for the best solution in each situation. Similar distortions of work have been observed in prioritizing tasks of the police and elderly care givers (Forssell & Ivarsson Westerberg, 2014).

But the fact that monitoring can affect how a task is performed is not a new phenomenon. It exists in all organizations. That pupils and students study more to pass exams than to learn for life is an ancient observation. That people are present at meetings is no guarantee that they are loyal or that they are absorbing any information. Nor is it certain that the person who talks the most in meetings is the one who works most efficiently or that the researcher who has published the most articles is the best researcher. It is easier to measure quantity than it is to measure quality, a drawback that can affect the monitoring of many tasks. If organizations focus on quantitative measures, they may prioritize productivity at the expense of maintenance work or focus on measurable limited efforts rather than genuine long-term results.

If it is not possible to monitor everything, would it be better simply to trust people?

Trust and Distrust

Trust is a concept that became widespread in the social sciences relatively recently – around the same time as the concept of networks. And that is no coincidence, because, as discussed in Chapter 3, relationships in the form of networks are often thought to be based on trust. But trust has also gained increasing use in theories of organizations, often as a critique of a one-sided emphasis on the importance of monitoring and control: It is often said that more trust is needed, that trust should replace the constant creation of new and uncertain methods of monitoring, that people in organizations could facilitate collaboration by trusting each other, and that trust would save many of the resources that go into monitoring (McEvily et al., 2003). From that viewpoint, monitoring is seen as an expression of distrust that is 'corrosive of human bonds – it is social acid' (Carey, 2017, p. 2).

But trust and distrust are connected. Instead of being an obstacle, distrust can be understood as a prerequisite for trust. In the first chapter of his book on the audit society, Michael Power (1997) wrote: 'What we need to decide as individuals, organizations and societies is how to combine checking and trusting' (p. 2). Trust, Luhmann (1997) argued, is directed towards the future (p. 20). When people declare that they trust someone in an organizational context, it is usually because they believe the other person will be able to accomplish a task with care and without cheating. But trust is always a risk. As Luhmann noted, 'Trust reduces social complexity, that is, simplifies life by taking a risk' (p. 71). One can never be completely sure of having made the right assessment, and even if one has had good reason to trust someone else, people can, for various reasons, fail to keep a trust or be forced to betray a trust. It is rarely a question of simply trusting someone or not. Rather it is a question of degree: What is the nature of the trust issue, how large is the risk, and how much can the person be trusted? 'Even the truster must retain a modicum of distrust – he must, for instance intervene if his colleague gives an opinion which is obviously false' (p. 93).

Thus, trust is reminiscent of decisions. Decisions are also directed towards the future; it is never entirely certain that decisions will have the intended effects. But whether making a decision or questioning if someone can be trusted, it is beneficial to have as much knowledge as possible to reduce uncertainty. In contrast to trust, monitoring always applies to something that has already happened. There is really no contradiction between trust and monitoring, therefore. Trust can be built up through previous monitoring, and the results of monitoring can provide good opportunities to assess whether someone can be trusted. Thus, organization provides good opportunities to trust people. In organizations, the issue of trust and distrust is depersonalized; there are different ways of checking on people, and individuals in the organization 'place their trust in the functioning of this distrust' (Luhmann, 1997, p. 92).

There are others who have decided that people can and should trust their colleagues. They simply must trust them because they are employees of the same organization, even if they have never met. The existence of locked spaces is an expression of distrust, but the assigning of keys or codes to locked spaces is an expression of trust. In this way, 'zones of trust' are created, in which the people who have access to them are expected to trust each other (Papakostas, 2012, p. 44).

SANCTIONS

Sanctions can be applied to encourage actions that lead to good results or to prevent bad behaviour; they can be either positive (the carrot) or negative (the whip). Positive sanctions are an obvious element in the social bonds of employment. To be employed is to receive compensation for a job, usually in the form of salary or wages. Although individuals may be dissatisfied with the financial remuneration they receive, employment is an instrumental exchange relationship. Wages can be calculated in various ways in the interest of fairness or to motivate workers; remuneration can be hourly, monthly, or performance-based. The determination of remuneration engages many actors; it is not merely an agreement between the individual employee and an employer. States can legislate on minimum wages, and unions can participate in wage negotiations. And employees can go on strike in an attempt to increase their income.

Another possible positive sanction for employees is the opportunity to develop a career – a significant element in Weber's (1968) bureaucratic model: The official 'expects to move from the lower, less important and less well paid, to the higher positions' (p. 963). By offering employees the opportunity for jobs with a better future and higher remuneration, many employers expect to create stronger motivation and identification with the organization's goals (Hechter, 1987, p. 143). Even in military organizations, career opportunities are a significant form of positive sanction, which takes place through competition. As Sundberg (2015) wrote of the Foreign Legion, 'Promotion in the Legion is based on members competing among each other, and the competition becomes harder the further up the ranking system one climbs' (p. 174). But if opportunities to compete for promotion are perceived as unfair, the legitimacy of the organization's hierarchy is in danger of being undermined. The employee of the month award is another type of positive sanction that some employers implement to generate what they see as a healthy competition among their employees. But for this strategy to work, there must be clear criteria for the award if employees are to know what they need to do so they can work accordingly.

Even if employment is governed primarily by positive sanctions, there can be negative sanctions such as wage deductions or warnings. And the ultimate negative sanction that social bonds can be cut is always in the background as a threat to most employees. As Hechter (1987) noted, 'Exclusion is the ultimate sanction in that it denies individuals access to the jointly produced good that they value' (p. 50). And even if a state has legislation restricting an employer's right to dismiss employees, dismissal is never completely banned.

The conditions regarding sanctions are similar in principle for all employees, whether they are employed in a company, a voluntary association, or a government agency, although there may be less risk of being fired from a federal job. But for members of voluntary associations and for most citizens, the bonds are constructed differently,[2] and offer few decided positive sanctions. The efforts that members make for their voluntary associations offer no compensation other than the sense of satisfaction derived from contributing to the organization. But if members misbehave in a way that can disrupt or discredit the association's activities, they can be excluded.

Citizenship is another social bond with few positive sanctions. Citizens may, to varying degrees, have social rights such as the right to vote or the right to health care. But rights are not sanctions; they are rules or laws. In both states and voluntary associations, positive sanctions are limited to awards of various kinds. In voluntary associations, members who have made great contributions to the organization over long periods can be appointed honorary members and may be exempted from paying membership fees in the future. States may award medals to citizens who are considered to have made particularly commendable contributions; in some states, citizens can be knighted. It is customary that prizes and awards are handed out publicly on special occasions in front of an audience of other members, so that as many people as possible can see that achievements can be rewarded in this way (cf. Sundberg, 2015, p. 177).

States have few positive sanctions available in the bonds to their citizens. Nor can they exclude them. When people embezzle money from their company, the company can fire them, but only the state can subject them to legal judgement and punishment. Cutting the bonds to people who do not fit into the organization or do not live up to expectations is a relatively comfortable way of avoiding problems. Because states cannot do this, they have developed a large repertoire of negative sanctions administered by courts and prisons that decide on the design of specific negative sanctions and the implementation of the sanction (cf. Foucault, 1979).

NOTES

1. There is some hesitation in the social sciences about seeing states as organizations. But although they are often referred to as institutions, many others seem to take it for granted that states are organizations. In the introduction to his book, *Coercion, Capital and European States*, Charles Tilly (1992) argues that states have been 'the world's largest and most powerful organizations for more than five thousand years' (p. 1). Yet political scientist Francis Fukuyama describes various states as both institutions (2012, p. 450) and organizations (2015, p. 23). Supporting the idea that states are organizations is the attention to and research on failed states (Rotberg, 2004). Organizations often fail but continue to exist despite those failures. Not so with institutions.
2. This reasoning is reminiscent of Etzioni's (1961, chapter 1) distinction among coercive power (threats), remunerative power (gained through material resources), and normative power (gained through symbolic rewards) over people occupying lower positions in the organizational hierarchy. According to Etzioni, coercive power is used in prisons, remunerative power in companies, and normative power in universities.

5. Bonded actions

In Chapter 1, I addressed the importance of understanding human actions as social – that human actions are oriented towards other people in response to what they are doing. Non-social actions, on the other hand, are performed without the involvement of others, as when an individual dons a warm sweater or goes jogging in the woods. But in order to understand why a person acts in a certain way in a certain situation, it is helpful to distinguish among forms of social action.

Although all social action is directed at other people, many social actions are initiated by someone who did not perform the action. The action is initiated by Person A but performed by Person B. I refer to this specific form of social action as *bonded action* – any action that is not a direct expression of the acting individual's will or decision – anything that someone asks, coerces, or forces another person to say or do. Bonded actions are, by definition, guided or controlled by social bonds. Other people may have expectations of what should be said or done or the way in which it should be said or done and may want to keep track of how the actions are performed and their results. Bonded actions are characterized by the social bonds that hold a relationship together, but the action itself can also be directed at people outside the relationship who may be included in other relationships.

And bonded actions seldom mean that the actions are entirely predetermined by the social bonds. Many bonded actions require some creativity – a dimension found in all human action, even actions that are described as routine (Joas, 1996, p. 197). The performance of bonded actions requires that Person B can understand what is expected, can perform the specified actions, and be able to put a personal stamp on how the action will be performed. The space and possibilities for the personal expression or design of bonded actions can vary but can rarely be eliminated. People can do the same things in surprisingly different ways, and it matters who is performing the action: which teacher, which doctor, which bus driver, or which baker. Social bonds provide people with motives, goals, knowledge, and resources to act, but it still must be people who act. People give life to a relationship through their bodies, their voices, and their emotional expressions. Without people, nothing happens.

Not all social action is bonded, but a large part of our everyday actions are performed within the framework of our various relationships and initiated by or together with others. And others keep track of these actions, whether visiting friends or relatives, shopping for food, or negotiating political deals or big business contracts. An invitation to a wedding or any other social event involves a great deal of bonded action. A friend or relative (Person A) initiates the action by sending an invitation to various people with whom that individual has a social bond. Person A decides when and where the guests (Person B, Person C, and so on) should appear. The inviter may decide the attire to be worn and where each guest should sit at the dinner table. Attending a wedding is definitely a social action, but with strong elements of bonded actions. Even if someone did not have a great desire to attend the wedding, it would be difficult to refuse the invitation without risking a damaged relationship.

Some social actions are not bonded – actions that no one else has requested, actions for which no one will question what was done or how it went, and actions that have no significance for a continued relationship. When people meet in public places and start talking to each other, the interaction can be facilitated if they follow common norms, but it does not become a matter of bonded actions if the actors do not know each other. Everything is happening for the moment, and no promises are made about the future; these actions concern no one but those who are currently interacting – talking, dancing, or making a purchase.

Through bonded actions, people's actions are linked together and can far exceed the individual's ability to act. But this connection does not have to occur through direct interaction, for more people to be doing the same things at the same time; it can also occur because there are others who continue and complement someone else's previous actions. Bonded action always involves a certain number of restrictions on freedom of action. But on the other hand, unimagined opportunities for action arise, which means that people can participate in and experience things they could never do on their own, such as flying to the moon or becoming world champions in football.

That actions are bonded means not only that they are initiated by or together with others within the same relationship, but often that people are provided with resources to help them perform these actions. They can have access to tools, instruments, machines, or other equipment that increases their ability to act. They can be helped to cope with things or provided with backup if someone fails or continues what someone else has started. Within a relationship, people can be trained and educated to perform actions they would have difficulty learning on their own; they have the opportunity to see how others perform those actions and are able to share trade secrets and methods specific to the relationship.

Bonded actions occur in all types of relationships, but the effect of coordination is strengthened and can occur on a larger scale through organization. Organizations can involve more people, the people are interchangeable, and organizations can arrange a long-term activity. Through organization, a larger number of actions can be linked together for a longer period. In this way, actions are arranged in a long chain of processes that create macrosociological effects. As Stinchcombe noted, only by 'growing the same way for a long time does anything get to be the size needed to produce macrosociological effects' (1985, p. 573).

People who act on behalf of organizations are transformed into *organizational centaurs* (Ahrne, 1994). In mythology, centaurs are animals with human heads, and it is said of them that their human characteristics are insufficient to restrain their animal nature. It is the same with the organizational centaurs: Their individual human features are insufficient to restrain the collective power of which they are a part. When interacting with organizational centaurs, one must bear in mind that they do not have any opinions or values of their own and that their emotional expressions are governed by the organization to which they belong. They have difficulty making their own decisions or making agreements; they must always ensure that they are doing the right thing or ask for permission. They are seldom spontaneous; they can be sluggish but come back with unimaginable force.

Organizational centaurs are treated differently by their external environment, depending on the organization to which they belong. The attention or respect they receive is due not primarily to their personalities, but to their organizational affiliations: Presidents from more powerful countries, directors from large companies, politicians from large political parties, and journalists from large newspapers receive more attention and find it easier to make themselves heard than do their less prestigious counterparts; their connection to organizational resources provides them with better treatment. In addition, access to resources can give them the power to get other people to do what they want.

THE DIVISION OF ACTIONS AND EMOTIONS

All relationships have a focus defined by their social bonds – not merely work organizations or voluntary associations, but also friendships; people do different things with different friends, for example (Ahrne, 2014, pp. 104–105; cf. Simmel, 1950b, p. 326). Most people are affiliated with several relationships, and they perform different types of bonded actions. In this way, the individual's ability to act is divided into pieces, and each piece uses only part of the person's repertoire of action. People enter relationships with only parts of themselves (Cooley, 1909, p. 319), because bonded actions provide space for certain qualities and skills of an individual, while others are hidden or neglected. Social bonds make use of parts of a person's energy and thinking, but the extent to which this is true varies greatly among relationships and the extent to which the individual sees it as a sacrifice or an opportunity.

It is not only actions that are divided and exercised in different relationships, but also emotions. Social bonds often include norms and rules for which emotions are appropriate in which contexts and how those emotions should be expressed. In the sociology of emotions, a distinction is made between the experience and the expression of emotions; how emotions are experienced and how they are expressed can vary from one relationship to another. As Hochschild (1983) argues, social bonds contain not only display rules – rules about expression; they also contain rules about feelings. During their upbringing, people learn different ways of dealing with their emotions, how those emotions are experienced, and how they should be expressed, and their expression can be suppressed or altered in several ways, depending on the situation. Emotions of joy or anger, for example, are expressed in different ways with the family, among friends, on a football field, or in a seminar room. As Bergman Blix (2015) has noted, 'Emotions are always managed' (p. 3).

ZONES OF BONDED ACTIONS

When people enter and are linked to a relationship, they must accept the reality that others will influence some of their actions and emotions – a phenomenon known in organizational theory as the *zone of indifference* (Barnard, 1968; Stinchcombe, 1990). This zone of indifference includes the actions that people expect their organizations to decide upon: 'The person affected will accept orders lying within this zone and is relatively indifferent as to what the order is' (Barnard, 1968, p. 169). The zone can be extensive and delimited by social bonds and is thus a matter of bonded actions. In some workplaces, employees have accepted the reality that their employer decides how they should dress (perhaps in uniform) and wear their hair, whereas people in other workplaces would react strongly if the organization were to make such demands upon them. Teachers have accepted that the principal decides which classes they are to teach, but teachers would be unlikely to accept an order to clean the school, because cleaning is clearly outside most teachers' zone of indifference. But a zone of indifference can change with circumstances and become the subject of negotiation or conflict. A person's zone of indifference can change as that individual becomes more powerful, and it can change as new people occupy positions of power in the organization.

The bureaucratic model (see Chapter 4) presupposes that the zone of indifference is both sharp and clear, and that it must have the same scope and design for everyone in the same position, so that the performance of tasks does not depend on who handles a particular case at a given time. As Weber (1968) highlighted in his discussion of bureaucracy, 'Bureaucracy develops the more perfectly, the more it is "dehumanized", the more completely it succeeds in eliminating from official business love, hatred, and all purely personal, irrational and emotional elements which escape calculation' (p. 975). The handling of a case must be predictable. Individuals who turn to an organization for assistance want their cases to be treated equally and not be dependent upon the person they happen to contact.

Weber's (1968) model may present an extreme strategy, but the importance of the principle of clear demarcation of expectations for the people occupying a certain position in a large organization is applicable in many types of organizations. The tension at the interface between individuals and organizations is always latent – not only in extreme bureaucracies such as authorities or insurance companies, but also in service or care professions that involve contact with customers or patients.

Social bonds define something that corresponds to a zone of indifference in all relationships, even if it is not always as sharp and clear as in an organization with many strict rules. But perhaps it is not always accurate to speak of a zone of indifference. People may not be completely indifferent to their options yet be willing to accept and fulfil expectations that they do not like. In that case, one could refer not to a zone of indifference, but to a *common zone* that includes the actions that others have the right to engage in or make demands upon.

In the case of states, the common zone refers to what citizens accept and expect the state to decide upon – how much a state has the right to interfere in the lives of its citizens, whether matters of free speech; the bonds between parents and children; or restrictions on the use of alcohol, tobacco, and cannabis. Questions about the content and scope of social bonds are often the subject of political conflicts.

In most friendships, the common zone is probably quite small. In most families, on the other hand, it is much larger and richer in content. The common issues can differ greatly, ranging from decisions about the purchase of a common home to the way family members are expected to express their feelings for each other. And the scope of the common zone can be controversial in the relationship of two spouses and in the relationship between parents and children. But not even in families is an individual's involvement total. There is life outside the family, and family members usually have other bonds in the form of work, friends, and hobbies.

But how are the interfaces drawn between what is and is not covered by the social bonds and bonded actions? What happens to those parts of an individual that do not fit in or are in demand by any social bonds? What tensions can arise between bonded actions, what does not belong there, and what should be left out? And how are the interfaces constructed between the different types of bonded actions performed by the same person?

THE INTERFACE BETWEEN INDIVIDUALS AND BONDS

Individuals are not equal to the sum of their social bonds. There is a tension between the part of an individual that is used in a social bond and that which is not in demand; what is left out is still somewhere in the background and cannot be completely ignored. And bonded actions that take place on behalf of others leave their mark, making an impression on the acting individual's body and soul.

In Erving Goffman's sociology, there are approaches to analysing this tension and what happens to the parts of a person that are not needed, exploited, or valued in a relationship. In the introduction to his 1959 book, *The Presentation of Self in Everyday Life*, Goffman shows the duality that can be found in people's performances in teams; on the one hand they perform the actions expected of them, but on the other hand they can perform these actions in a way that expresses something more, perhaps something other than what is expected. Goffman calls expected actions *expressions given* and those not expected he labels *expressions given off*: 'The second involves a wide range of actions that others can treat as symptomatic of the actor' (p. 2).

In his later work, Goffman uses other terms for the same phenomenon (cf. Burns, 1992, p. 137). In *Asylums*, he discussed *secondary adjustments*, which stand for the various ways in which a person stands apart from what is expected (Goffman, 1968, p. 172). He notes that secondary adjustments are covered partly by such established notions as 'informal' or 'unofficial'. Goffman (1971) also introduced the concept of *role distance*, which he describes as 'the divergence between actual performance and obligation' (p. 102). Role distance is not necessarily an expression of distancing from what people do together; it can just as easily be a creative addition to the interaction in a relationship that transcends the limitations of social bonds. Such creativity may be necessary for two people to cope with difficult tasks together, as in Goffman's analyses of the collaboration between doctors and nurses in a complicated surgery (pp. 108–113).

Even when people do not wholeheartedly embrace their bonded actions, the body is always involved, which is a critical part of Hans Joas' (1996) theory of creative action: 'corporeality shows itself to be the constitutive precondition for creativity not only in perception but also in action itself' (p. 163; see also Joas & Knöbl, 2009, p. 518). No action can occur without bodies, and bodies are indivisible; human beings cannot participate in a social bond with parts of their bodies. Even for a factory worker who performs one-sided movements using only certain muscles during work, other parts of the body are affected, which can eventually lead to injury and disease. Bodies are a source of strength, but they are also vulnerable. They have many characteristics, which are differentially significant in different contexts. Therefore, various aspects of the human body often have great relevance for creating the interface between the individual and the bond. When establishing social bonds, some bodily aspects can be integrated into what is expected, whereas others can stand out. And bodies change and age.

An implicit assumption has been made in traditional role theory: that it is possible to distinguish between the role and the person – that a role is merely a role. But the person who holds a certain role always matters. With his reasoning about role distance, Goffman (1971) highlights the factors that make the concept of role problematic. Even if we imagine that people play roles in their relationships and that the social bonds define the role that a person is expected to perform in a certain relationship, it is almost impossible to separate the role from the person. It is people rather than roles that comprise relationships and social bonds.

Casting

Casting refers to the selection of actors or performers for parts of a presentation. It is associated primarily with film and theatre – in which case it refers to the placement of people who are suitable for a specific role. Various highly specific aspects are usually crucial: age, sex, body shape (slim, fat, athletic, tall, short), skin colour, and various characteristics of appearance or voice. But specific personality traits and difficult-to-define qualities such as charisma can also be sought. Through high-quality casting, the space and need for acting is reduced, because the actor has already demonstrated many of the qualities that the role would require.

But casting occurs not only in film and theatre. There is a major difference between actors and other people in the casting context: Although most people's roles are long lasting, actors change their roles frequently. Casting can be understood as a method of creating greater correspondence between individual and bond, which makes it easier to construct social bonds, by looking for people who form a fit in as many respects as possible, even in aspects that are not directly relevant for the tasks at hand.

Some form of casting occurs in most social bonds. When it comes to appointing people to represent a political party, physical characteristics such as age, gender, or skin colour are often given great weight. The emphasis on and argumentation for the importance of these factors may vary, however; it is often implicit or so obvious that it is not discussed. In the search for or establishment of romantic love relationships, there is also a strong element of casting, in which people are quite explicit about the physical characteristics they expect in a potential partner.

When it comes to employment in companies or other organizations, the selection of people takes place primarily in relation to tasks that are relevant and based on skills, education, experience, and qualifications. When the selection among the applicants for a job is made, however, there are often other types of wants and expectations about aspects of the applicant that are not directly about education and professional experience. When recruiters emphasize the importance of a personal meeting, it may not be so much a question of checking out details in the person's CV, but rather a desire to see the candidate in real life. Exactly how the applicant answers questions in the job interview may even be of secondary importance. Organizations want people who fit in in a general sense and fitting in can be about anything from personality traits, social skills, and health to such characteristics as age, sex, appearance, and skin colour – significantly larger sections of an individual than mere specific skills.

As noted, bodily characteristics can sometimes be integrated and become parts of a social bond, but sometimes they stand out and are not relevant. One aspect of corporeality that receives a great deal of attention in both public debate and research is sex. Sex is an aspect that can be utilized in a social bond and be less relevant in other contexts. In many work situations, employers and sometimes employees make a clear division between positions that are suitable for either men or women (cf. Acker, 2006). Sometimes some employers may exploit female sexuality in shaping a position such as club hostess in a restaurant or nightclub (Cockburn, 1991, p. 149). In many other contexts, the division between male and female jobs is not explicitly conscious; it may be unspoken, albeit obvious to the employer. And employers who want to demonstrate equality in hiring and promotion may emphasize that sex does not play a role in their decisions.

In recent years, research on work organizations has drawn increased attention to employers who try to create a visual identity through the specific physical appearance of their employees as a strategy for profiling their company (Huzell, 2015). This strategy may be a determining factor in the recruitment of employees for the service sector and for 'front stage' (cf. Goffman, 1959, p. 107) staff members who have direct contact with guests and customers.

An early expression of this insight is given by C. Wright Mills (1951) in his book, *White Collar*, in which he describes a certain type of young female salesperson: 'She attracts the customer with modulated voice, artful attire, and stance' (p. 175). In research, this phenomenon is referred to as *aesthetic labour*: 'the aesthetic labourer might be seen as an animated component of the scenographic aesthetic of a service organization' (Witz et al., 2003, p. 50). Some researchers have described *lookism*, which indicates that employers rate the physical attractiveness of employees and job candidates and prefer people perceived as physically attractive. One way for employers to select the candidates they think look best is to request that jobseekers submit a photo with their job application (Warhurst et al., 2009).

Aesthetic labour means that bodily aspects – often a combination of characteristics in demand by employers – are strongly integrated into the social bonds. And this is not merely a preference for women or men; rather physically attractive young women or men with a certain skin colour have preference. Exactly which properties fit can vary considerably and depend on the circumstances. As Mulinari (2007) reported, a restaurant in Sweden that focused on Indian food recruited several young women of colour as waitresses. But they were not allowed to stay when the restaurant switched to serving Swedish home cooking.

Greedy Relationships

Efforts are made in some relationships to ensure that much of what the participants do becomes bonded actions, by prohibiting other bonds or making them more difficult to establish. People in such *greedy relationships* are not 'content with claiming a segment of the energy of individuals but demanding their total allegiance' (Coser, 1967, p. 198). This strategy is practised in such voluntary organizations as religious sects and monasteries and in military and paramilitary organizations such as the French Foreign Legion and criminal gangs. Some companies also try to use this strategy by creating a strong organizational culture and identification with the company.

That monks or nuns should live in celibacy could be interpreted as an expression of greediness; their convent lives are not to be disturbed by any other bonds. And 'tagging' gang members with tattoos of the gang's symbols is a way of embodying gang affiliation. Coser (1964) outlines an even more extreme case of greediness: Some organizations have used body mutilations to achieve that effect – by castrating men to create eunuchs, for example.

Contacts with people outside a relationship can be made more difficult by the demands placed on those involved: 'Distinctive diet, dress, grooming, and social customs constrain and often stigmatize members, making participation in alternative activities more costly' (Iannacone, 1994, p. 1188). One example is the military. Soldiers in the French Foreign Legion must wear their uniforms on and off duty, for example, an order that Sundberg (2015) contends 'signifies organizational greediness, as members must always appear as members for outsiders' (p. 137).

The fact that organizations try to engage as much of their members' lives as possible by banning other social bonds need not necessarily be combined with long-term bonds. For limited periods, other organizations can also be greedy, as experienced by players on a national team at a training camp or during a crucial tournament.

Emotion Management

Experiences and expressions of emotions are another aspect of corporeal participation in social relationships, and adolescence is the time when most people learn to control their emotions to some degree. The way one experiences and interprets those emotional impressions is significant, but perhaps even more relevant is the way one expresses emotions in different contexts. The way people experience their emotions and how they show them to others is often part of the social bonds connecting them to their different relationships.

In everyday speech, people often talk about emotions as genuine or false, but it is probably more accurate to suggest that individuals learn to understand and reinterpret their emotions in different situations. Ever since Arlie Hochschild's (1983) book, *The Managed Heart*, was published, *emotional labour* – the different expectations of people's emotional expressions in their work – has become a subject of a great deal of research (Wharton, 2009). Hochschild's book was based mainly on research on flight attendants' emotional labour, but other research in the field has been based on different types of service work.

Bergman Blix (2010) has studied actors as a professional group for which different forms of emotional work are central. Through her research on the way actors rehearse their roles, she has gained an understanding of emotional labour as a process – how the emotional expressions that actors display on stage or screen have been shaped and learned. Based on her study of actors, Bergman Blix has developed a model for learning and practising emotional labour – a development of Hochschild's (1983) reasoning about an over-involved worker who mixes private and professional roles and an emotionally distanced worker who fails to engage in the professional role. This model has been applied in a study of emotion management among judges and prosecutors.

In her study of how actors learn their roles, Bergman Blix (2010) clarified: 'Their starting point is their own private emotional experiences, but during rehearsals they turn them into professional expressions' (p. 59). This process can be described through decoupling: One captures a feeling that is familiar by drawing on previous experiences but changes how it is expressed, depending on the situation in which it is to be displayed. It is necessary for actors to find a connection, an emotional path, between their own emotions and how those emotions can be expressed. Such a process of emotional work was also found in the study of judges and prosecutors. Without such a connection, there is a risk that emotional expressions will lose their meaning (cf. Kolb, 2011). At the same time, these new ways of expressing familiar emotions are easier to turn on and off.

The process of recreating previous emotional experiences and giving them new expressions requires increased self-control in the emotional path. That new emotional expressions are strenuous and energy-intensive was shown in the study that compared new and more experienced judges: Habituation occurs when the situation-adapted emotional expressions become habituated and can occur without conscious effort, thereby providing increased security and an emotional presence (Bergman Blix & Wettergren, 2018, p. 19). Because professional emotional expressions are based on previous emotional experiences, they also constitute an investment of the self in the professional situation. So it is not merely about going in and out of different roles, because they are connected and can influence each other. There can be situations in court work that are particularly emotionally demanding – cruel crimes, for example, can cause 'dramaturgical stress', which causes the new emotional expressions to get out of play (p. 168). Then the interface between individual and bond can break down.

THE INTERFACE BETWEEN BONDS

I have discussed how the interface between individuals and bonds can vary. In this section, I describe the tensions that can arise in the interface between different bonded actions when they are performed by the same individual. For many people, their bonded actions are about different types of chores. They may have a family and a job and may be part of a voluntary association or a religious community. Being included in such a set of bonded actions does not necessarily create any substantive clashes or overlaps. For the individual, however, collisions can occur regarding time. It may be problematic or almost impossible to fit all the schedules together. There may simply not be enough time for anything other than bonded actions.

For many types of relationships – and the family is a perfect example – there are strong expectations that the same person should not be included in more than one relationship of the same kind. That the same person would be a member of several political parties or religious communities would not seem credible either; nor can one be a member of two football clubs at the same time. In these contexts, one expects a correspondence between the individual and the bond. Anything else would not only seem strange – in order to protect the interface between bonds – it may not even be allowed.

Most people only have one citizenship. But with an intensified globalization in the form of migration, and an increase in travel with various forms of study abroad, more people have become citizens of two or even more states. But there are still several greedy states – China, Japan, and Iran, for example – that do not accept their citizens being citizens of any country other than the one in which they were born.

Some people are born with dual citizenship because some states have provisions for an innate citizenship and apply various combinations of *jus soli* (citizenship in country of birth) and *jus sanguini* (citizenship of parent) (cf.

Chapter 3). People who emigrated to the USA in the 19th century became naturalized citizens after a few years. But many countries of origin were against this process and forced people to choose between becoming a US citizen and maintaining their previous citizenship. It was assumed that dual citizenship would decrease loyalty to the state. One issue was military service – that a person should not belong to the armed forces of two different states (Spiro, 2017).

But in recent decades, more and more states have accepted the existence of multiple citizenships and see it as an opportunity for bilateral contacts. This development has also created opportunities for wealthy people to obtain additional citizenship through investments in other countries, which can be advantageous for their taxation. A continued increase in the prevalence of multiple citizenships may someday change the very meaning of citizenship, however (Baubäck, 2019).

But there is no acceptance for multiple citizenship in sports – especially not in team sports. There are strict rules about the country a player can represent in the Olympics or other world championships, and it is usually virtually impossible for a player to change countries, even between different championship tournaments. One cannot compete against oneself. But there are no restrictions on the citizenship of coaches at this level of sporting events.

Belonging to different relationships of the same kind can give rise to questions about a person's loyalty. But there may be other problems with overlaps and clashes between a person's various bonded actions that are not primarily a problem for the individual but are a problem for the relationship – relationship-specific secrets, for example, or access to collective resources of various kinds. Furthermore, when individuals break the bonds with a relationship and move to a new one, overlaps between the old and the new social bonds can be problematic.

Secrets

In most relationships, there are secrets about which insiders do not want the outside world to be privy, either because the secret is embarrassing or because it would degrade reputations if it became public knowledge. But there are also secrets from which others could benefit: a secret recipe perhaps or a code to a locked door. In a relationship, one constantly strives to maintain a facade to the outside world, which seldom completely agrees with what that relationship looks like from the inside. Goffman (1959) described how a married couple, or as he called it, 'a marriage team', behaves to 'sustain the impression new audiences expect of it' (p. 79). In organizational theory, it is said that an organization strives to protect its inner core (Thompson, 1967) by explaining what one does in a way that lives up to the expectations of the environment (Meyer &

Rowan, 1977). Such behaviour is universal and applies to all types of relationships from families and friendships to companies and states. Those involved in a relationship also expect each other not to ruin the external impression, because it would also affect the person who failed to 'sustain the impression'. But the duration of such expectations of loyalty and silence depends largely on the other bonded actions in which the individuals are involved. And that can change over time. Tensions between different social bonds can become strong if major economic interests, ideological interests, or strong emotions are at stake.

But the fear of secrets being leaked also depends on the level of interest those secrets generate in the external environment. Not all gossip is interesting. Few people outside of neighbours and close relatives are interested in hearing family gossip unless the people involved are famous, in which case the gossip may be worth money to newspapers or book publishers. It has become common in marriages between wealthy celebrities to enter a confidentiality provision into their prenuptial agreements to try to ensure that details of the marriage do not leak in the event of divorce (Garfield, 1997).

Many companies are partially protected from leaking their secrets to competitors through patent law and the protection of certain intellectual properties such as trademarks. But in their activities, there are often different types of trade secrets that are not protected – confidential information such as a process, a technique, or a compilation of information that gives the company 'an actual or potential economic advantage over others' (Garfield, 1997, p. 269). To safeguard such trade secrets, employees or even certain customers can bind themselves or sell their silence by signing a contract of silence. Such contracts can be relatively far reaching and cover most of what an employee has become aware, whether technical details and information about individuals that could damage the relationship or a company's reputation and opportunities.

There are many derogatory epithets for those who reveal secrets, ranging from gossipers to traitors. But there is also a word that has a strong positive connotation: whistleblower. A whistleblower is often seen as a hero who dares to reveal unpleasant truths despite the risk of retaliation. Definitions of whistleblowing usually include the idea that it is a matter of the revelations serving a generally good purpose and that the revealer's actions were based on good intentions (Arnold, 2020; Haglunds, 2009; Stanger, 2019). But in discussions about the concept of whistleblowing, it is also emphasized that what serves a general purpose is not always obvious, as is clear from the title of Henrik Ibsen's (1882) play, *An Enemy of the People*, a drama about a physician who revealed that the water in a spa was toxic, a revelation that incited the anger of the locals. Stanger's (2019) study of whistleblowers in the USA suggests that they 'are all too often commended for speaking truth to power, and then persecuted for it when media attention has moved on' (p. 9).

The most famous case of whistleblowing in Sweden occurred when an engineer employed at the armament factory, Bofors, revealed bribes in several large international armament affairs, and the smuggling of arms to banned countries in the Middle East. These revelations attracted general attention and horror in Sweden and internationally. But the employees and residents of the small town in which the factory was located reacted to the whistleblower with disgust (Haglunds, 2009). Whistleblowers are often portrayed in the mass media as lone heroes who go against the flow, but the situation is not usually that simple:

> There may be a lone, heroic (or not so heroic) protagonist at the center of a case – a single individual who initiates an episode of secret-spilling. But with few exceptions each case involves, at a minimum, that individual plus a recipient/publisher of the secret. And there are often more people and organizations involved – facilitators – who work on the receiving end or somewhere in the middle. (Arnold, 2020, p. 191)

In the Bofors case, the revelation was preceded by the fact that the engineer who revealed the secrets had become a member of the Green Party, which was strongly critical of Sweden's arms exports (Haglunds, 2009).

Control Over and Access To Collective Resources

Corruption and nepotism are two phenomena that can occur when people who are involved in a relationship and who control or have access to some type of collective resources exceed or go outside the social bonds to connect to social bonds within another relationship. Nepotism occurs when the bonds to one's own family or relatives trump the social bonds to an organization. It could be a civil servant who fixes jobs for relatives rather than hiring the most deserving people, or a politician whose children are given high posts in the party.

Corruption is a broader concept that can include a variety of bonded actions wherein people exceed or abuse their position within a relationship in their contacts with people who are outside the relationship or involved in other relationships. Much of what we define as corruption occurs through new bonds that arise between representatives of different organizations – often transactions between states and companies (cf. Stanger, 2019, p. 90). The more openings that arise in the boundaries between states and companies, the greater the opportunities for corruption (Castillo, 2013).

Such relationships can begin as friendships; people meet in other contexts and have contact with each other professionally, perhaps in negotiations of major contracts. Trust is developed gradually in a corrupt relationship (Papakostas, 2012, p. 107). The parties get to know each other; they know what they want from each other; and they trust that they will get it. And they trust that the newly established bond is exclusive and secret.

Company representatives with resources at their disposal may offer dinner or send Christmas presents. But such gifts can sometimes give rise to suspicions of corruption; the norm of reciprocity implies that the recipient of a gift is expected to give something in return (cf. Chapter 2). It does not have to be based on common agreement, because the mere acceptance of a gift or an invitation to dinner is an acknowledgement of willingness to engage in reciprocity. Many states limit the value of such gifts – how much a civil servant may receive without being considered corrupt. In the USA, such an understanding of corruption has long been a guiding principle in legislation, but this position has gradually changed in recent years. For something to be regarded as corruption within the meaning of the law, it is now required that it be a direct exchange of benefits (Teachout, 2014).

Another form of corruption is match fixing in professional sports. The purpose is to be able to win big money by betting on unforeseen results in a match. But winning requires that one or more players in one of the teams be involved. One method used by match fixers is to offer to sponsor a club, while simultaneously gaining the opportunity to recruit players. When they succeed in bringing in players with whom they already have bonds, they can influence the matches and fix the results. The best situation for a match fixer in football (called soccer in North America) is the opportunity to recruit a goalkeeper. Match fixers can also keep track of players in a team. If they discover someone with a gambling addiction, they can offer to lend that person money. The loan becomes difficult to repay, and the player can be easily manipulated.

Breaking Bonds

When a person leaves a relationship, the pressure from the others involved to maintain silence about former internal relationships or secrets is no longer as strong. Thus, many contracts of silence pertain not only when the individual is an incumbent but continue to apply after the person has left the relationship. But when someone leaves one workplace for another, the revealing of internal secrets is not the only danger. The larger question is whether these individuals bring knowledge with them that can be used in the new relationship. In this way, competitors can gain access to knowledge that may not be confidential, yet difficult to access. In such cases, it is not merely an individual who is recruited, but part of the organization from which that person comes. The knowledge may also come in the form of contacts with customers or suppliers. When a book editor moves to another publishing house, the authors with whom that editor worked will usually move too. To avoid this loss of resources, there are various types of agreements, contracts, and quarantine provisions that limit employees' opportunities to use their former employer's resources in a new relationship – that they may not take a job in their industry for one or two years after leaving their previous position, for example. This restriction is especially relevant if their employee has given the person who leaves highly specific training. The possibility that such people should quit when their training is completed reduces employers' willingness to pay for further training for other employees.

Employees' moves from a government job to a company position have received some attention in recent years. Politicians who move to better-paying positions in lobby companies or government officials in such ministries as finance, defence, or energy, can be recruited to companies in matching industries – companies that benefit in their operations from a knowledge of state policies. In many states, quarantine provisions apply to such transitions, but they are seldom particularly far reaching or extensive. In an overview of this transition pattern in the USA, Stanger (2019) concluded, 'When moving from government service to a position as a lobbyist or contractor has become a socially acceptable steppingstone to wealth, the question of who is overseeing and serving whom can have no clear answer' (p. 192).

In the world of sports, especially team sports, club changes are tightly regulated with special transition periods and opportunities to borrow players for a time. In professional football (soccer) and ice hockey, buying and selling and trading players is an accepted business model; a large part of the work consists of training towards improvement – training that other clubs are willing to pay for. It is only logical, therefore, that in order to receive a dividend from such an investment, these clubs can sell the player to another club for more than they originally paid. A professional football or sports club is an extreme example of how an organization's resources are invested in an individual, but one may ask why this business model is not applied by other companies. Could computer companies sell their programmers to other companies, and could states charge when politicians are hired by lobbying companies? Could universities claim a transfer fee when a successful researcher moves to another university?

In the next chapter, I examine how millions of people in clusters of social bonds form the social landscape around them by repeating their bonded actions.

6.   A striped world of relationships

People's social bonds are linked to different types of relationships – not to a specific society (cf. Chapter 2). Through social bonds with different forms, people who live or work in different parts of the world can maintain contact, collaborate, and keep track of each other without direct interaction. People can be citizens of one or more state, they can belong to a family whose members live in several continents, and they can be employed by companies that have their operations spread across many countries. Social bonds can create a social closeness that bridges large geographical distances.

In the social sciences, however, it is still said that the world is divided into a number of separate societies. Researchers compare these societies and label them developed or undeveloped, democratic or authoritarian, industrial or post-industrial societies. One reason for this deadlock in the alleged importance of distinct societies is the strong connection of the social sciences to states. Social scientists are expected to provide data to the state administration in the form of national accounts; demographic data on marriage, divorce, and childbirth; crime statistics; data on the population's health and general well-being; and political preferences.

If one assumes that the world is divided into a number of separate societies, one risks an exaggeration of the homogeneity of one's own 'society' and the differences compared to other 'societies'. What is seen as typical of a society can, on closer inspection, turn out to be rooted in a mixture of impulses, phenomena, and experiences from many quarters. If a society, a certain geographical territory whose borders are controlled by a state, is categorized as post-industrial, it probably does not mean that all companies within this territory have ceased to engage in industrial production. Any reference to a post-industrial society occurs because the industrial companies in the country have moved their production to other countries (cf. Chapter 4). To explain how these companies work, one must go beyond the country's territorial boundaries and ensure social relations, regardless of geographical boundaries. If there are limits to the analysis of a relationship to a country, there is great risk that one does not see the whole relationship and therefore obtains a skewed picture of what holds it together, how it changes, and how significant it is. In addition, it has been shown that the idea that a country should be characterized by a certain type of company is greatly exaggerated. Rather, most countries have several types of companies that represent different production paradigms (Lane &

Wood, 2009). There are varieties of capitalism both between and within countries.

States are not societies. They are a type of relationship based on territorial boundaries. A state tries to have some control over its own citizens and territory, but there are large variations among states in the degree of influence they have over events within their borders and how they exercise this influence. There are also a number of failed states (Rotberg, 2004).

But states matter. In most states, there is a tendency for homogenization of relationships through legislation, education, language, culture, and historical traditions. Relationships that transcend a state's boundaries are affected by local conditions in the states in which they operate. Spatial proximity is not insignificant. Even if individuals have not established direct contact with their neighbours in a residential area or in a small village, it is difficult to ignore them. Geographical proximity usually involves certain common interests in dealing with the shared environment, which gives rise to interaction at regular or irregular intervals. But the important thing is not to take homogeneity for granted, but to recognize that it can vary among states and times. The starting point must be that really homogeneous societies are exceptions that must be explained (cf. Robertson, 2014, p. 29).

The mixture of relationships that converge in a particular country or part of a country can be understood as a social landscape, in which phenomena with different characteristics (such geographical landscapes as rivers and mountains, meadows and forests, cities and villages) spread in various directions become dependent upon each other for their local affiliation, even if the main activity is not local at all. The landscape metaphor has gradually crept into various social science reasoning as a replacement for such concepts as system or structure (see e.g., Ahrne, 1990; Djelic, 2014; Mazzucato, 2014; Pierson, 2000) to denote a more or less temporary constellation of phenomena spread differentially over time and space. A landscape has no boundaries; the horizon shifts as one travels through the landscape and gains new perspectives and sees other constellations. The different parts of a landscape change at different rates. A social landscape consists of constellations of relationships that cross each other without any common logic but which at least temporarily become dependent on each other in the same way that 'the operations of elements in the natural world' can give rise to 'a range of different permutations and distinctions with elements existing independently or combining and recombining in many different ways' (Lane & Wood, 2009, p. 540).

On a world map, we see the world divided into some 200 more or less square countries of different sizes, which are considered separate societies. But with intensifying globalization, these boxes are increasingly crossed by narrow corridors of relationships that stretch through a large number of these boxes. The world is becoming more striped than chequered.

In the next section, I discuss how these stripes, or global compartments of activities, can be created and maintained. I examine a few ways a relationship can be expanded and spread in the social landscape, while being simultaneously held together. I then describe how organizations with no previous permanent contact with each other can form meta-organizations to gain increased control over their environments and create favourable conditions for their joint activities. In this way, organizations can enter into global relationships without having to relocate their operations.

In the following section, I describe and analyse what happens in the interaction between different relationships when they encounter each other in the social landscape: how they interact with each other, how they position themselves towards each other, how they constitute each other's surroundings, and how they try to form their own and others' environments. A relational social analysis cannot look merely at what happens inside relationships but must also examine what happens outside them and how, together, in competition, or in struggles with each other, they strive to shape their environments.

If there are no societies, how are we to understand social change? I discuss this question in the third and concluding section of this chapter. Rather than assuming that entire societies change, we can analyse change by looking at the conditions for the emergence of new relationships and how they affect existing relationships. We must understand social change by looking at the dynamics between old and new relationships.

GLOBAL RELATIONSHIPS

The concept of globalization was introduced surprisingly late in the social sciences (Stearns, 2020). One of the first to make use of the idea was Anthony Giddens (1990), who defined globalization as 'the intensification of worldwide social relations which link distant localities in such ways that local happenings are shaped by events occurring many miles away and vice versa' (p. 64). During the 1990s, a number of books on the subject of globalization appeared (e.g., Albrow, 1996; Robertson, 1992; Sklair, 1991).[1]

That the 1990s saw such a great interest in globalization was not strange, even though the phenomenon itself did not suddenly arise at that time. Technological innovations that improved and intensified opportunities for different types of communication across the globe made it inevitable to talk about globalization. It has always been wrong to describe the world as divided into different societies, but then it became more wrong than ever. Since the 1990s, globalization has been further intensified and has penetrated into everyday life through increased opportunities for people to communicate directly with each other over long geographical distances.

As many social scientists opened their eyes to the phenomenon of globalization, they realized that it was nothing new. There are various suggestions as to how far back in history one can go to find when globalization began, but it is obviously related to what one means by globalization. But if we take a long view of human history, to see how humanity has spread over the earth, the realization that the world is connected is more correct than assuming that the world consists of various autonomous societies. How countries and states have arisen and demarcated their borders must be examined and problematized and should not be taken for granted.

Globalization has taken place in various more or less intense phases (Stearns, 2020). It is not a unified process; rather, one could talk about the plural – globalizations (Mann, 2013, chapter 1). We need to disaggregate the concept of globalization to recognize that it comprises many phenomena from migration and trade to the spread of technological innovations and religious teachings, which occurred in different ways and at different rates.

Both Global and Local

Ever since social scientists began to discuss globalization, there have been various suggestions about its causes and effects. There has been talk of Westernization and of a convergence that could lead to countries becoming more and more similar. This view has been criticized, however, in favour of an emphasis on 'glocalization', which 'refers to the process by which phenomena that spread, flow, or are diffused from one "place" to another are adapted to the new locality where they arrive' (Robertson, 2014, p. 28).

Globalization is often described as a diffusion of phenomena through what can be called the travelling of ideas – a spread based on people becoming aware of or seeing how others do something and trying to do the same thing elsewhere. Perhaps someone visits another country, takes an idea home, and tries to realize it there. Or perhaps people move and take ideas with them that they apply in their new home. And the subject of the travelling ideas can be anything from religious teachings, political ideas, or a new sport, to an industrial manufacturing process. Because travelling ideas often need to be translated (Czarniawska-Joerges & Joerges, 1996, p. 13-48) in order to fit them into a new environment, their dissemination does not obviously lead to increased convergence. Anyone who brings an idea of what a certain organization should look like, for example, has considerable leeway in presenting the idea and how it should be realized in the new place (Ahrne & Brunsson, 2014). How the idea takes shape and the timing of its actualization depends on the other relationships that are in place. As Tilly (1984) noted: 'when things happen in a sequence affects how they happen' (p. 14).

If we analyse globalization from the perspective of relationships, the question of the relationship between the local and the global will be different. Relationships are rarely completely local; they can usually be extended spatially; they connect people who are in different places. That's the key to relationships: They do not spread from one place to another; rather, they expand and connect places. At the same time, various resources can accompany their expansion, and previous local conditions can be disturbed in a way that differs from the way a spread takes place through the travel of ideas. The most important thing to understand is not a comparison between two places where the idea is then found, but how the new bonds are formed.

The Expansion of Relationships

Migration is rarely about individuals. It is usually a spatial extension of kinship. When one or more family members moves to another country for whatever reason, kinship relations remain, even if the bonds change. In fact, the move to another country to study or work is often planned and financed by the entire family. In a study of current migration and academic education, Forstorp and Mellström (2018) use the term global 'eduscapes'. They emphasize that migration 'with higher education as the driving force is not something that only concerns individuals but is also part of extensive family and kin stories' (p. 83). Migration of this type is a form of bonded action, and the family keeps track of how the studies are going.

Many migrants send money to relatives who remain at home – remittances that are part of the continued social bonds rather than mere financial transactions. It is a gift-relationship based on notions of long-term reciprocity (cf. Chapter 3). As Åkesson (2011) noted:

> The repayment that senders may anticipate is never explicitly defined but they may expect to be attended to with care and respect in their contacts with receivers and to be rewarded with a prominent role both in local and transnational family life. (p. 344)

The conditions for spreading and expanding activities differ among types of organizations and other relationships. Given their strong territorial ties, states have relatively few opportunities to expand their activities; some attempts are made, albeit no longer to the extent they were 50 years ago. Mafias are difficult to export and tend to be local in scope. A mafia organization's reputation for violence is built around an environment with strong ethnic and family-based relationships, a situation I discuss later in this chapter, and which also applies to political parties. As Varese (2011) explained, 'As a rule political (and criminal) reputations are local and are the products of costly investments' (p. 191; cf. Catino, 2019).

Unlike states and mafias, companies constitute a type of relationship that has many opportunities to spread its activities over large distances (cf. Chapter 4). But like the case with families, corporate globalization is about expansion rather than relocation. A company can move its production to another country in order to buy cheaper labour or to bring production closer to its customers, but it is unusual for the head office to be moved as well. It is not surprising, however, that a relationship such as a corporation conducts its business in different places. It often happens within one country that a company is head-quartered in a major city, whereas production is spread to different parts of the country. There are also a number of voluntary associations, such as the Red Cross and Amnesty International, that have expanded by establishing new branches in other countries. What is noteworthy from a relational perspective is what the continued social bonds look like, whether they are within the same country or in many different countries.

Increased opportunities for companies to expand globally give them an advantage over states. And they are not merely looking for cheaper labour or increased proximity to consumers; they are often escaping their country's leg-islation regarding everything from employment relationships to tax legislation. There are currently more than 75 states (many of them relatively small) and partially independent jurisdictions around the globe that are currently referred to as tax havens. But they are characterized not only by low or non-existent taxes, but also by secrecy provisions and light and flexible incorporation of foreign businesses (Palan et al., 2010).

The ways of expanding a company's operations differ in the nature of the continued relationships. The form most commonly associated with corporate globalization is the multinational corporation (Morgan et al., 2001), which means that the same company has expanded, but that the decision-making power of the company still lies with the old owners. But multinational compa-nies can be created in more than one way. The company can establish a com-pletely new organization in a new place that is reminiscent of the company's organizations elsewhere. IKEA is a typical example of that strategy (Torekull, 1999). But a multinational can also expand by buying up local companies. This often happens among companies in the food industry such as Unilever. (See Jones, 2005.) Because many attempts at globalization run the risk of encountering opposition from locals, acquired companies usually keep their name as a way of trying to hide the globalization that is occurring and avoiding a 'liability of foreignness' (Zaheer, 2002).

Another model for expanding a company's business is franchising, which is a form of licensing whereby a parent company gives another independent company the right to do business in a prescribed manner. When spreading through franchising, one can expect some differences among companies that are basically doing the same things. Franchising creates constant tension between the desire to maintain global brand uniformity and allowing sufficient autonomy to respond to local market demands (Rosado-Serrano et al., 2018).

McDonald's is probably the world's most famous example of franchising. Research on McDonald's has shown that their concept of a fast-food restaurant has been abandoned in many places. In some places there is even table service and candles on the tables; in other places McDonald's functions as a café where people can sit for long periods and talk (Watson, 1997).

The opposite of what happens through franchising is the creation of great but hidden similarities, allowing companies that cooperate to retain their own names and brands and remain independent – a situation that exists in many so-called interfirm networks. Describing these collaborations as networks suggests that they would be relatively loose and unsystematic. But if one looks more closely, one often finds that they are partially organized. Such interfirm networks are common among airlines. Star Alliance, for example, was established in 1977 with 5 members. At the beginning of the 2020s, the number had increased to 26. The requirements for becoming a member are strict, new members are carefully examined, and members monitor each other according to a list of 85 criteria, such as safe travel and customer benefits and handling (Sydow, 2019).

Meta-organizations

One reason there has been a tendency in organizational theory to see organizations as subordinate to a social structure and to see organizations as a meso-level between micro and macro may have been the focus on individual organizations that are seen as exposed to such strong pressure from their environments that they have no choice but to adapt. But researchers have overlooked the fact that organizations can be organized; they do not have to fight alone against an overpowering environment. Meta-organizations are a form of collective action for organizations that allow them, by working together, to take command of parts of their environments and create suitable rules and conditions for their businesses. Organizations are not only, as North (1993) assumed, players who follow ready-made rules – they also make their own rules.

Meta-organizations are associations, but members can be other types of organizations, such as companies or states. Membership is voluntary, and members have the full right to leave the organization as they see fit. Meta-organizations are comparatively easy to form; potential members are usually well known, and not many members are required at the beginning. Membership in a meta-organization is usually based on a certain similarity of the members: They can be companies in a certain industry, sports associations in a certain sport, organizations such as universities with a certain type of activity, or organizations with a nonprofit activity. Their similarity facilitates the collaboration, and in the long run a membership tends to make the members more similar to each other. Meta-organizations can look quite different; there is no ready-made model, no institution – consequently, no norms or expectations – for how a meta-organization should be designed. The number of global meta-organizations has increased rapidly since the end of World War II and has contributed to the global expansion of many types of activities. Of more than 10,000 international meta-organizations that were registered in 2003, 90 per cent were formed after 1950 (Ahrne & Brunsson, 2008).

Through membership in meta-organizations, organizations can participate in a process of globalization without having to move or change their boundaries (Ahrne & Brunsson, 2014). Almost all companies are members of a national trade association, which is also likely to be a member of a worldwide meta-organization. Meta-organizations do not produce anything, and they have few external contacts, but they do create global corridors of cooperation, even between competing companies. These global meta-organizations, such as the International Federation of the Phonographic Industry (IFPI) and the International Federation of Pharmaceutical Manufacturers & Associations (IFPMA), are often unknown outside of their industry, but are of great importance to companies' global contacts. One purpose of most trade associations, whether national or global, is to influence states to adopt measures favourable to the industry or to protect the industry from measures that could have a direct negative impact upon them (Dumez & Renou, 2020, p. 106).

Meta-organizations play a crucial role in most competitive sports, and meta-organizations organize world championships and other types of championship competitions. In the vast majority of sports, there are meta-organizations like Fédération Internationale de Football Association (FIFA) and International Judo Federation (IJF) that decide about rules and how tournaments and competitions should be organized. There are few other modern activities that are organized down to the smallest detail through membership, monitoring, rules, and sanctions to the extent that global elite sports are organized.

But there are global meta-organizations in most areas of activity: International Cremation Federation, International Egg Commission, World Ostrich Association, BirdLife International, International Association of Universities. Because meta-organizations are often unknown to anyone other than to their members, the visibility of the global compartments that they form is small; it is the members who are visible.

The Internet is a global compartment that a large portion of the world's population accesses today, but we do not see how the Internet is governed; it seems to be connected through some magical power. But the Internet is primarily governed by two meta-organizations: the Internet Society, founded in 1992;

and the World Wide Web Consortium (W3C), founded in 1994. Many of their dealings are with standardization – ways to make the network cohesive. W3C is a meta-organization with more than 400 member organizations, including universities, government authorities, and small and large companies with interests in the computer industry. The Internet Society has five membership categories – Platinum, Gold, Silver, Bronze, and Copper – depending on the cost of membership fees paid. Different categories are given different benefits and levels of influence. The Internet Society also has individual members.

In recent decades, a number of meta-organizations have included members with greater differences than usually exist in meta-organizations: the Forest Stewardship Council (FSC) and the Marine Stewardship Council (MSC), for example (Tamm Hallström & Boström, 2010). In these so-called multi-stakeholder organizations, members often consist of both companies and voluntary associations, which try to create rules about collaboration in certain activities. These rules often address environmental issues and sustainability: problems that are characterized by complexity and that provoke confrontation of values and require a collective solution (Dumez & Renou, 2020, p. 108).

States represent a type of relationship based on a territorial connection, in terms of both citizens and tasks. Historically, states have tried, and sometimes succeeded, in forcibly expanding their territories through war and coloniza-tion. But, fortunately, over the last 50 years, this form of state enlargement has almost ceased. In the world of the 21st century, the vast majority of wars are within states, and any increase in the number of countries on the planet has occurred primarily through division. For states, membership in meta-organizations has therefore become an increasingly critical part of their activities, providing them with opportunities for direct influence over what is happening in other states, while simultaneously creating opportunities for other states to influence their agenda. Membership in a meta-organization can create increased opportunities for interaction and exchange in the form of, for example, trade, education, and tourism. In addition to such well-known inter-national meta-organizations as the United Nations (UN), the European Union (EU) or the African Union (AU), there are a large number of meta-organizations that focus on specific government activities – one example being the Universal Postal Union (UPU), which was formed in 1874 to facilitate universal postal services. Three examples of relatively unknown meta-organizations for gov-ernment activities are Interpol, the World Customs Organization, and the International Criminal Court.

Despite their importance, meta-organizations have significant weaknesses as organizations. The foremost organizational element in meta-organizations is membership. In most meta-organizations there are also rules, sometimes in the form of voluntary standards. Many meta-organizations are partially organized and lack hierarchy or have a weakly developed hierarchy and no real monitoring or sanctions of their members (Berkowitz & Bor, 2019; Berkowitz & Dumez, 2015).

Meta-organizations often operate in silence but with great perseverance. They may have difficulty making decisions, and their decision-making processes are lengthy and uncertain. Total unanimity or near-unanimity is often required. This is especially obvious in large, well-known meta-organizations such as the UN or the EU. A meta-organization cannot encroach too much on the members' independence or identity (Ahrne & Brunsson, 2008).

Meta-organizations are some of the most frequent drivers of globalization. But there is a big difference in the success rates of meta-organizations that can be largely explained by two factors: how dependent the members are on their membership for their activities and the extent of the meta-organization's resources. Following are two examples from the fields of sports and politics that illustrate these differences.

The idea of how to play football spread from England during the second half of the 19th century, through people studying in England or through English workers who stayed in other countries (Giulianotti & Robertson, 2009; Sugden & Tomlinson, 1998). Local football clubs were eventually formed in many parts of the world. During the same period, the idea of establishing socialist parties spread rapidly around the world, through migrant workers and activists who travelled from country to country. This migration resulted in a number of parties with quite different designs and programmes (Eley, 2002). But both football clubs and socialist parties aspired to act globally.

FIFA was formed in 1904 by 7 European countries. Its expansion in world football has not been without conflicts and opposition, especially from South American associations (Dietschy, 2013). But even though FIFA's organization has gone through several crises, this meta-organization has, in the long run, strengthened its position and has been able to create a global corridor of football with its own economic principles, its own rules, and a great deal of power (Sugden & Tomlinson, 1998).

Socialist parties have also made several attempts to create global meta-organizations in their goal of realizing the famous words of Marx and Engels: 'Workers of the world unite.' The first time was in 1889 with the Second International, which split during World War I. In 1951, Socialist International (SI) was formed as a meta-organization for parties with a democratic socialist ideology. SI has had major problems, however, in the form of disagreements between members, and demands have often been made to exclude certain members (Ahrne & Sörbom, 2020). The Liberal International has also had similar difficulties (Smith, 2001).

The differences between the massive global success of football and the great difficulties of political parties in forming meta-organizations that span the globe can provide an understanding of what is required to create viable global corridors. By deciding on common rules for all the clubs and national teams around the world, FIFA has enabled an interaction among its members in different types of tournaments to nominate world champions or champions for specific continents. FIFA has created its own global space and is now a meta-organization with large financial resources, thanks to its revenues from the sale of TV rights to major football tournaments. In addition, FIFA's members are completely dependent on their membership for the ability to participate in various championships.

In the world of football, there is a fragile balance between the global and the local. The local connection of professional football clubs provides them with an identity, even though the players may come from many countries. Thus, local supporter clubs are important in maintaining the balance between the global and the local. But not even supporters are local anymore, because most people watch football on TV rather than watching live games in real life. A club like Manchester United has many millions of supporters in Asia, for instance (Giulianotti & Robertson, 2009, p. 144), and supporter clubs also form meta-organizations (Cleland et al., 2018).

When it comes to politics, it is quite the opposite: The local and national arenas weigh much more heavily and become dominant. Despite their membership in SI, socialist parties in different countries find it difficult to interact with each other – but neither has that been their most important goal. The primary goal for every SI member is to win elections in its own country. In order to have the opportunity to do so, it must take a stand on a number of national political issues, leading to a split. The socialist parties that are or have been members of SI have had constant conflicts over their most diverse issues, such as abortion, environmental issues, and international issues. The local becomes the central, making it almost impossible to achieve cooperation across national borders. The members' broad and strong national rootedness means that they remain too different, even though they share a common ideology.

This strong local dependence of political parties also applies to parties with other ideological orientations. The globalization of politics has not been able to keep up with 'some of the other facets of globalization' (Stearns, 2020, p. 165). Successful globalization seems to require specialization. Global compartments are narrow and cramped. In politics, this can be seen in such successful organizations as Amnesty International and Greenpeace, which focus on specific relatively limited political issues. The difficulties that political parties face in becoming global actors provide opportunities for enterprises to engage in global politics – as members of the World Economic Forum, for example (Garsten & Sörbom, 2018).

BETWEEN AND AMONG RELATIONSHIPS

In this and the following section, I change perspectives. Rather than discussing how relationships can be held together and expanded, I explore how they relate to each other. Organizations and other relationships are dependent upon exchanges with others and have developed various methods for doing so. In this discussion, I focus primarily on organizations, which organize not only what happens inside, but also organize their external environments, although often only partially.

The interaction between organizations in the social landscape is governed not by overarching systems or structures, but by human decisions. If there are no systems or structures to create order, organizations must do it themselves. But no organization is superior to any other, although they may have different levels of access to resources that provide power and opportunities for persuading others to do as they want.

Power resources can take various forms, and they are not always comparable (Mann, 2013, p. 428). Power can be in the background without being noticed. No actors really know how much power they have – much less how much power others have. For the actor who wants to exercise power, it is important to create the impression of having access to large power resources. But it is better to be able to get one's goals realized without having to use and consume one's power resources, as there are costs associated with that strategy (Etzioni, 1968; Korpi, 1985). Threats can be enough to make other actors believe that they are prepared to use their power. Actors doing as others want them to do can happen simply out of habit. One's perceptions of others' power resources and abilities to intervene may become outdated. Power resources can change and diminish even if they are not used: weapons can become obsolete and members' loyalty and motivation can decrease. The problem is that the only way to find out about another party's power is to enter into open conflict – to challenge the power. Etzioni (1968, p. 319) has emphasized that if it were really possible to measure power in advance, there would be few violent conflicts breaking out, because the outcome would be a given and known in advance.

But not all success depends on power; success can depend on skill or perhaps luck, or both – to have the opportunity to realize the right ideas at the right time. It is not power that has made big computer companies like Apple, Google, or Facebook successful, as I elaborate upon in the next section. But their success has given them power resources that they may not really know how to use today.

The spaces between organizations and other actors are described in some social science research as fields. A field is defined as a constructed social order in which actors interact with each other on the basis of a common under-standing of what the interaction is about and how it should proceed (Fligstein & McAdam, 2012). A field can arise when two or more actors with similar objectives 'are compelled to take one another's actions into account' (p. 167). A field can thus be understood as an open social relationship (cf. Chapter 1). Instead of focusing on a field, it therefore becomes more interesting in a rela-tional perspective to start with the actors to see what they do with each other. The actors create the fields and not the other way around. In the next section, I discuss how organizations try to organize their environments and their con-tacts with other organizations. I then discuss three modes of interaction among organizations and other relationships: collaboration, conflict, and competition.

Organization Outside Organizations

Institutionally, states differ from other organizations. States are expected to have control over their own territory and an ability to govern the country and create order. Weber (1968) argued that states can be distinguished from other organizations by their 'claim to the monopoly of the legitimate use of physical force in the enforcement of its order' (p. 54). In addition, states have a monopoly on taxation. In a relational perspective, on the other hand, states have no priority over other organizations. Like other organizations, states are constructed through combinations of social bonds, and what states do happens in the form of bonded actions, whether by police officers, soldiers, judges, kings, or queens. States have other power resources at their disposal that most organizations do not have. Are states more powerful, then? It is difficult to generalize about their power and strength, because there are such enormous differences among the world's approximately 200 states. To understand what states do and their significance for organizing what happens within their terri-tory, Fukuyama (2015), who has made a comparative historical analysis of the organizational forms of states, has proposed a distinction between state scope and state strength. Scope applies to what a certain state has the ambition to perform and strength applies to its ability to perform what it has planned to do. Few states have both considerable strength and a comprehensive scope. Other states have relatively limited scope but significant strength or vice versa. And a not-insignificant number has neither (pp. 59–63).

These huge differences among states cannot be explained institutionally, so an explanation must be sought in centuries-old historical sequences. Favourable for the development of both strength and scope seems to have been the ability of a state's administrative organization to be stabilized before politi-cal modernization and the extension of suffrage (Papakostas, 2018). Fukuyama (2015) contends that the development of each state is 'neither a deterministic process nor an entirely voluntaristic one, which is why it must be studied in its full historical context' (p. 557). And there is seldom any unambiguous explanation as to why a state has received its specific design, but it is 'a result of a concatenation of accidental events, in which actions had unintended consequences' (p. 556).

Few states have an absolute monopoly on the use of physical force, and in some states, there are strong restrictions on the way the country's power resources can be used. A state's collective power resources can be extensive, but they must be spread out and used in many contexts. States are expected to do a variety of things, and, according to political scientist Charles Lindblom (1977), a state's power resources render it clumsy in certain ways. Yet, states – especially the largest and most powerful states in the world – can do things that other organizations cannot. Their resources allow them to take large risks. They can start wars or launch spacecraft. They can also be the first to explore and develop new technology. Economist Mariana Mazzucato (2014) has shown how many states have 'provided the main source of dynamism and innovation in advanced industrial economies', and they have 'kick-started and developed the engine of growth in areas such as aviation, computers, and green technology' (p. 8).

What is common to all states, however, is the change in the power relations between states and companies that has taken place with globalization and which has given companies increased opportunities to move their operations and their money from one state to another. What happens can be summarized with Sassen's (2006) short phrase: 'States today confront new geographies of power' (p. 222). As the relationships that exist within their territories increasingly extend outside their borders, it becomes more difficult for states to monitor and compel others to follow their decisions. This applies not only to companies, but also to criminal gangs, and even families.

Corporate environments are often described as markets, and a market is thought to emerge spontaneously through the interaction of companies and customers. In order for exchanges in markets to work, however, a great deal of organization is often required in the form of many rules and much monitoring; markets are, to a significant extent, partially organized (Brunsson & Jutterström, 2018). There can be various actors who organize markets: states; companies through their meta-organizations; and voluntary associations that can, for example, decide on rules for environmentally friendly products. These actors can make decisions about goods to be exchanged, activities or characteristics of the seller or buyer, and the ways in which exchanges should be handled and even prices should be set (Ahrne et al., 2018).

In their interaction with customers, most companies are partially organized. Customers who visit a store are monitored. Restaurants may have rules for how their guests can dress. Audiences in theatres, cinemas, or sports arenas are checked before they can enter to see if they have bought tickets, and visitors are sometimes inspected for certain items that they cannot bring into the establishment. Museums have guards in the halls who monitor how visitors behave, and the queues formed by people who want to be admitted are often organized as well (Ahrne et al., 2019). There is a great deal of organization even outside organizations.

Visitors are usually anonymous, however; they do not have to provide a name and address when buying something in a store or visiting a museum. But it has become increasingly common for retailers to offer their customers a membership allowing them special deals and providing them with discounts if they register their purchases. Then customers must provide their name, phone number, and address or e-mail address, so they can be reached with advertising. But as long as there is no selection process and no requirement to make certain purchases or to spend a certain amount of money, it remains an open relationship.

Other organizations offer and organize open relationships. Political parties organize demonstrations and meetings; sports associations can arrange competitions, such as races in which people participate more for exercise than prizes – races in which non-members can participate; religious congregations can welcome visitors to their meetings. But in most cases, participants in demonstrations, races, or religious gatherings are monitored to ensure that they are following certain rules, and they can be rejected if they fail to do so.

Although open relationships can be partially organized, there are no social bonds – no commitments and no promises to return. A customer who goes into a store does not have to buy anything and does not promise to ever return. A person who attends a political meeting does not promise to vote for that party in the next election. But that does not mean that all social bonds are dissolved. In the interaction between an employed salesperson and a customer, both salespeople and customers can act on the basis of their social bonds. Salespeople have certain expectations from the employer, their work can be monitored, and they may receive bonuses if they manage to sell a certain amount. Customers may also act in accordance with their bonds to their family or their company. There may be people who want to know what they bought and what they paid for it. But in the interaction between sellers and customers, there are no bonds, for there is always genuine uncertainty as to whether there will be an exchange.

Companies that are involved in monitoring other companies, such as the credit rating companies Moody's and Standard & Poor (now S&P Global Ratings), also serve as examples of partial organization outside organizations. Other companies, like Guide Michelin and The World's Fifty Best Restaurants rank restaurants around the world. The awarding of Nobel Prizes and Oscars are other examples of positive sanctions that constitute attempts to govern the world through partial organization. In recent years, as Edlund et al. (2019)

report, there has been a virtual explosion in the number of awards being offered in a variety of areas.

Collaboration, Conflict, and Competition

Organizations are shaped in interplay with their environments. Where one organization should begin and another end cannot always be taken for granted, and these borders can change over time. Instead of interacting with other organizations, through exchanges of goods or services, for example, organizations can try to fix such things themselves by bringing in more members with different skills. And organizations can sometimes merge, or they can split. It is a fundamental issue for all organizations to decide which form is optimal – how big they should be and how many different things they should do. In theory, there are two answers to this question. The first answer points to the relationship itself as an obstacle to incorporating more activities; there may be a risk that the relationship becomes too complex and that it becomes difficult to create and maintain social bonds that cover a large number of activities (cf. Luhmann, 2018, p. 253). The second answer has to do with the environment and the extent to which an organization can access what it needs – the transaction costs to gaining access to the components necessary for the business. If exchanges with other relationships are easy to achieve and if there are many opportunities for such exchanges, transaction costs are low. Then it becomes unnecessary for an organization to include the making of these components or the performing of such tasks. If, on the other hand, it is difficult to create desirable exchanges, and especially if it is something that is particularly important for survival, transaction costs will be high. Then it may be relevant to incorporate this into the organization (Williamson, 1981). The size and form of a relationship rests on a balance between these two dilemmas: increased complexity or increased transaction costs.

An alternative could be *collaboration*. Through shorter or longer collaborations with other organizations, an organization can gain access to increased resources and competence without having to decide whether they want to grow or consider the risks of not getting what they need. Such collaborations often take place in projects; they differ from collaborations in meta-organizations in two main ways: (1) The members of most meta-organizations are the same type of organizations, and (2) membership in a meta-organization is long term and never time-limited.

Projects are often about unique and complex tasks that require different types of skills, and collaborations in projects have a beginning and an end. To quote Sydow and Braun (2018), the participating organizations have 'neither a past nor a future beyond the present collaboration' (p. 7), yet a successful collaboration can give rise to new collaborations in the future. Collaborative projects are common in traditional industries such as construction and consulting, but also in science-based industries such as biotechnology, film production, and music. Project collaborations may require new, temporary social bonds between individuals from the various organizations and they often have their own governance structure that differs from those of the participating organizations (Sydow & Braun, 2018).

Political parties can work together in coalitions or alliances, and collaborations between voluntary organizations often take place around temporary political campaigns. Sponsorship is another type of collaboration that often occurs between companies and another type of organization – a sports association, a voluntary association running a charity, or a museum. Even criminal organizations or gangs often collaborate in temporary projects for special coups (Rostami et al., 2018).

Another form of collaboration that often occurs globally is the value chains mentioned in Chapter 4. In these, a specialization takes place between different companies, which may mean that a company deals only with the design and marketing of its products, while contracting out the manufacturing. This way of outsourcing production to more anonymous companies has come to be known as Nikefication because of Nike's outsourcing reputation, but it occurs in many industries (Davis, 2016, pp. 72–73). In this way, the product's brand is not directly associated with the manufacturing or the working conditions that characterize it.

Even in collaborations, access to power resources can be critical. If one of the parties believes that it has more power and is less dependent on cooperation than the other party is, and if the other party shares this view of the power relations, the powerful-appearing party can dictate the terms in its favour. In this way, there may be a latent *conflict* that is not noticeable to outsiders. On the surface, everything can seem fine, but if the dissatisfied party believes that the power between the parties is becoming equal, the conflict may become open. The probability of open conflict is greatest when power differences are levelling out (Korpi, 1985).

But conflict does not have to mean that a collaboration or exchange ceases completely, as long as there is something to argue about – something that both parties are interested in getting or keeping. Simmel (1964) has written about conflict as a form of interaction: As long as the parties do not aim to destroy each other, it is

> almost inevitable that an element of commonness injects itself into the enmity once the stage of open violence yields to any other relationship, even though this new relationship may contain a completely undiminished sum of animosity between the two parties. (p. 26)

Despite the enmity, the parties must have some contact with each other and use their power resources strategically to be able to get the biggest slice of pie. But from the beginning, it is more effective merely to threaten with power resources, so as not to waste them. And in negotiations, the parties can talk about power and try to make their threats as credible as possible. But if open conflict goes too far, there may be other parties that can intervene to mediate. Traditionally, that has been a task of states.

Unlike collaborations and conflicts, *competition* does not involve direct contact between the organizations that see each other as competitors. Competitors do not strive to create opportunities for exchanges with each other. Simmel (1964) emphasizes that the goal in competition is rather to win 'the favor of one or more third persons' (p. 61). These third persons can be customers, but they can also be voters in a political election or students who choose which university they want to attend. As Arora-Jonsson et al. (2021b) have noted, 'Competition is one of the master trends in society.'

Competition can be understood as an open relationship between two or more players. According to Arora-Jonsson et al. (2020), a relationship is characterized by competition if some actors believe that there are other actors with the same desire and if they think that what they desire is a scarce good. The competition can be more or less obvious for different players. There is direct competition when those who compete with each other are aware of each other and observe and keep track of the actions of their competitors. But competition can be more diffuse if competitors are not really aware of each other. And competition can even be a one-sided relationship, if Player 1 sees Player 2 as a competitor, but Player 2 is unaware of being in a competitive relationship.

Competition can be about a wide variety of things; it often takes the form of competition for customers, prizes in a contest, status, or even attention. Not only companies are involved in competitions; many types of relationships such as families, social movements, or sports associations experience competition. Relational actors who see each other as competitors strive for the same things. Competition presupposes a certain similarity between those who compete with each other – that they see themselves as belonging to the same category of actors. Competition can vary in intensity over time. One can speak of an episodic competition as opposed to a continuous competition. Episodic competition in the form of contests is typical of sports, but contests also occur in other areas, in the form of political elections and of competitions among architectural firms for proposals for the construction of major buildings (Arora-Jonsson et al., 2020).

Competition is usually seen as positive, based on the notion that those who compete will make an extra effort and do their best to obtain their desires. But competition does not necessarily mean a particular type of action: 'Competition is a relationship that can give rise to actions; it is not the action in itself' (Arora-Jonsson et al., 2021a, p. 15). Some players may make an extra effort when they discover new competitors, whereas others try to put the brakes on their business. Competition does not exclude cooperation: Membership in a meta-organization, which is, by definition, cooperative, may sometimes be a prerequisite for participation in a competition, for instance.

SOCIAL CHANGE AND ORGANIZATIONAL CHANGE

It is usually assumed that social change is about changes that apply to a particular society, and that different societies are at different stages of development. Many labels have been suggested to characterize these stages: agricultural society, industrial society, service society, post-industrial or postmodern society, information society, or network society. Change is thought to mean that a society goes from one stage to the next. Periods of transition are seen as times of upheaval and are turbulent and troubled. But it can be worth the effort, for change is thought to imply that things get better – at least eventually. Social change is assumed to have a certain direction: forward and upward.

The slightly caricatured notion of social change I have presented survives as a taken-for-granted undercurrent in much of the social science research, despite being subjected to harsh criticism. It does not seem as obvious to many later social theorists, however, that social change progresses towards ever-higher stages. Piotr Sztompka's (1993) critique is summarized in a view of societal change that is 'purged of all evolutionist or developmentalist overtones; it does not assume any necessary, unique goal nor an irreversible course of historical change' (p. 140). And Joas and Knöbl (2009) emphasize 'the absurdity of the popular notion that history is linear' (p. 523). Another critique of traditional change theories notes that no 'prime mover' can be found to explain change – not economics, technology, ideologies, or other changes in values can individually explain processes of change (Mann, 2013, p. 439). Joas (2003) has criticized the idea that one can explain social change endogenously, merely by looking at what happens in a single society. He regards the tendency towards endogenous explanations for societal change as 'sociology's birth defect' which can 'prove fatal to the discipline and its credibility' (p. 54).

If we are to take thoughts and insights about the significance of intensified globalization seriously, a traditional notion of societal change will be impossible. One cannot characterize the world today with any of the terms that have been proposed to describe different stages of development; everywhere there is a mixture of the old and the new, and change can go in different directions. In a striped world, old and new exist side by side.

It is not possible to create a new society – only new relationships. But creating new relationships does not mean that the old ones disappear. To understand changes in the social landscape, one must examine the interplay between old and new relationships. In what follows, I first discuss why it is difficult to change old organizations and other relationships, why they are characterized by inertia, and why they remain. Next, I examine how the inertia of old relationships creates opportunities to establish new ones. Finally, I reflect on the interplay between old and new relationships.

Inertia

It is not strange that relationships are difficult to change – that they are characterized by inertia. Relationships are created in such a way that the participants can have something to come back to – something that seems stable, wherein they feel at home, know what they are expected to do, do not have to start from the beginning every time, and do not have to explain themselves. This situation applies to most relationships, from families and friendships to companies and states. If some of the bonds in a relationship are disrupted, it 'loses its form and character, its identity, its very existence as an ongoing entity' (Kaufman, 1995, p. xi).

There is a tendency in most organizations to do what they do best at the time, at the expense of future new opportunities (Ingram, 1998; March, 1991). The resources that have accumulated in an organization are designed for certain purposes, to enable a certain type of action. A change in what the organization is doing would risk losing these resources, for change can be a waste of resources, at least in the short term (Hannan & Freeman, 1989, pp. 71–72).

Because rules serve as organizational memory (cf. Chapter 4), major rule changes can mean a loss of key knowledge about the way to do things. As described in Chapter 4, it is also the case that many established organizations lack an ability to perceive problems and opportunities in their environment. In old organizations, language, routines, control systems, and information systems are created over time, based on certain types of observations and events but excluding many others. And for those who see new things in the environment, it may be impossible to convey this knowledge within the organization. Not least, a strong organizational culture or ideology contributes to such blindness to new phenomena. Their inherent inertia means that organizations carry with them traces of the time and environment in which they were formed (Stinchcombe, 1965), much like buildings from different decades exhibit similar architectural features.

Inertia does not mean that nothing changes, however; rather, it means that change is slow and happens in paths that have already been mapped (cf. Hannan & Freeman, 1989, p. 70). Most established organizations eventually adapt to changes that are taking place around them and incorporate new technical solutions to conduct their business, but it is rare that they completely change the direction of their activities. This point is nicely illustrated by Alfred

Chandler's (1962) conclusion in his study of big corporations in the USA: 'the nature of the company's original line and the resulting accumulation of resources determined the extent to which the new products could be developed and new markets captured' (p. 392).

In most industries, a natural selection of companies takes place over time. Those that succeed, survive, and gain a strong position and legitimacy that, despite their inertia, can secure their position. But it is far from certain that it is the most efficient organizations that survive (Hannan & Freeman, 1989, p. 37).

Age can be a clear advantage for organizations. Many organizations can count on increasing returns: Success breeds success and provides new resources. This truism applies to many types of activities, not least in knowledge-intensive sectors (Pierson, 2000). Most of the highest-ranked universities in the world have a long history. Even successful football clubs have a tendency to profit from increasing returns.

Many organizations can survive without really achieving their goals. One can speak of 'permanently failing organizations', which fulfil a valuable function, even without meeting the expectations and goals of the owners or the responsible officials and politicians (Meyer & Zucker, 1989). Whether they are schools that do not attract enough students or companies that receive grants to run an unprofitable business for labour market reasons, they may be almost impossible to close down. And in relation to the expectations and demands for what states should do, most of the states around the world can be described as permanently failing in certain respects (cf. Bromley & Meyer, 2015, p. 189).

Some organizations can survive for a long time with minimal resources, yet later, when given the opportunity, they suddenly have air under their wings and grow quickly. The Catholic Church in Poland and the Orthodox Church in Russia are two organizations that led a dwindling existence during the communist dictatorships but were given ample space when communism was overthrown.

Inertia is a form of change – perhaps the most common form. The slightly disturbing implication is that it is impossible for things to remain as they are forever; nor is change as radical and fast as many wish. Perhaps because organizations are characterized by inertia, there is strong pressure for rapid change. The popular organizational literature is flooded with ideas about how to create change (Du Gay & Vikkelsø, 2012). But most such attempts are far from successful (Brunsson, 2006). In Chapter 4, I asked a question: 'Is it possible to step into the same organization several times?' Based on the reasoning of organizational inertia, we would unconditionally answer 'yes' to that question.

But if we also know that the people who are currently attached to a certain organization are interchangeable, the answer will be less certain.

> Organizations constantly need vacancies, positions that have to be filled, if they are to undertake reforms or other innovations. But people do not age or die fast enough. New positions therefore have to be established, new departments set up, new organizations founded. (Luhmann, 2018, p. 255)

The organization, with its resources and rules, is like the riverbed that moves slowly, while the people who stream through the organization can come up with new ideas and renewed energy.

Innovation

Spontaneously, inertia is understood as an obstacle to innovation, but it is rather the opposite in the social landscape. Inertia can make room for something new. The inertia of old organizations is a precondition for the possibility of establishing new ones. When addressing innovation in general terms, it is almost always linked to the idea of creative destruction (Schumpeter, 1987). Basically, the theory of creative destruction is based on the assumption that long-standing arrangements and assumptions must be destroyed in order to free up resources and energy to be deployed for innovation. But if the inertia of old organizations means that there may be room for new ones, no destruction is needed.

The idea of *open spaces* can capture the historical temporality that arises in the coincidence of different organizational processes with different temporalities. Open social spaces offer historical opportunities (Ahrne & Papakostas, 2014). In areas already occupied by organizations, people and resources are bound to different social relationships, and the stronger and more multifaceted these bonds are, the more difficult it is to establish new organizations (Shefter, 1994; Stinchcombe, 1968). New organizations become organizationally out-flanked (Mann, 1986, p. 7) or 'out-crowded' (Markovits, 1988).

It is far from obvious, however, that the open spaces[2] that can exist around organizations lead to the formation of new organizations. And the fact that there is unused space cannot constitute the entire explanation for the emergence of a new organization. Open spaces are characterized by unpredictability. Surprising things can happen there; small initial efforts may be enough to achieve unimaginable results. Hopeless projects can have unexpected success and proliferation processes can have an accelerated pace. Organizations can expand, agitators can create mass movements, prophets can found churches. Open spaces can be regarded as 'dynamic social fields' (Sztompka, 1993), where processes of organization and reorganization can take place. From a historical perspective, the timing of the exploitation of such spaces and the organizational solutions that have arisen there have given the social landscape in different parts of the world their characteristic profiles.

Varying aspects of the inertia of old organizations provide a different type of open space (Ahrne & Papakostas, 2014). Distinguishing between open spaces provides an understanding of the interplay between old and new organizations. When old organizations neither see nor can utilize the resources around them, we can refer to *old open spaces*, which are seen as part of a natural order woven into the general inertia of social life. They are often discovered by chance and not infrequently by travellers and strangers who, in Simmel's (1950b) essay 'The stranger' are nearby yet distant. Tourist facilities in many parts of the world have been built in places that no established organizations had seen as open spaces with unexpected opportunities.

Abandoned spaces can arise when old organizations move or close down their operations (cf. Aldrich, 1999, p. 260). Resources can be left behind: people, buildings, even machines or natural resources, which can become resources for new organizations. Ancient castles and countryside mansions are being converted into conference facilities and golf clubs. Cheap airlines such as Ryanair have been made possible by obtaining space at abandoned military airports around Europe (Barbot, 2006). For the development of IKEA's business model, the opportunity to buy an abandoned factory cheaply in a town by the railway in southern Sweden was crucial (Torekull, 1999). The now-global online company, Amazon, had some of its first premises in abandoned warehouses on the outskirts of Seattle (Stone, 2013).

There may also be *forbidden spaces*, identified by organizations that are aware of the possibilities for new organizations in their vicinity but see them as undesirable or threatening. States may prohibit certain types of organizations within their territory. Companies can take measures to stop potential competitors through boycotts or other methods, or they may even use physical threats against employees who try to establish trade unions. Swedish furniture manufacturers boycotted IKEA for its sales methods, which is one reason that IKEA went abroad for its furniture production (Torekull, 1999). But if the bans are lifted, the *opened spaces* can quickly be filled by new organizations. In Sweden, private employment services were banned for a long time, but when the ban was lifted in 1993, the space created was soon filled by new staffing companies. Several of these new companies were already established in other countries, and they were quickly able to expand their operations. Some of them eventually collaborated with the state employment service (Ahrne & Garsten, 1998). The emergence and enormous development of the Chinese e-commerce company, Alibaba, can be understood, at least in part, in light of the spaces that opened up in China when economic policy changed towards the end of the 20th century. Alibaba was founded in 1999 and was able to offer

Chinese customers a completely different service than were the state-owned enterprises, which tended to see customers as mere inconveniences. Alibaba's banking operations also had room to grow rapidly, given the state banks' lack of interest in families and small businesses (Clark, 2016).

There are also *prepared spaces*, as when old organizations try to attract new organizations. States or cities can provide infrastructure such as roads or electricity or create special zones with lower taxes and duties to attract new businesses.

New organizations can be formed and grow in *shadowed spaces* (cf. Tilly et al., 1975). Old organizations can provide protection by offering premises and access to various resources. So student organizations grow in the shadow of universities and new companies grow under the protection of so-called incubators, which offer intensive, intangible, high value-added assets such as management, legal services, and networking opportunities (Barbero et al., 2014). This protection can be offered by other large companies, universities, or other research organizations.

Brand *new spaces* can also arise. Historically, urbanization has meant many new spaces. The migration of people from country to city provides a strong explanation for the emergence of several new voluntary associations in the late 19th and early 20th centuries, such as trade unions and sports associations. As cities have grown, open spaces have emerged in the periphery, where access to resources such as land and underemployed people has been greater (Hall, 1998, p. 302). IKEA had its big breakthrough in Sweden in 1965 when it opened a large department store in one of Stockholm's newly built suburbs (Torekull, 1999). The origin of McDonald's business and service concept was developed in the 1940s in a small restaurant on the outskirts of Los Angeles, with customers comprised mainly of families with children. The concept was then spread throughout the USA by a contractor who bought plots on the outskirts of major cities and built restaurant premises (Boas & Chain, 1976).

The establishment of mafia organizations can be explained as a combination of abandoned and new spaces. A mafia can arise in an area undergoing a sudden and late transition to a market economy in which there is no actor who can reliably protect property rights or settle business disputes. In addition, the establishment of a mafia requires that there be people available who have been trained in violence and have recently become unemployed. Such a space existed in Sicily in the first half of the 19th century, in Japan towards the end of the 19th century, and in the Soviet Union/Russia at the end of the 20th century (Varese, 2011, pp. 193–194).

New spaces are also emerging through technological breakthroughs. The most spectacular organizational innovations anywhere in the world in recent decades have taken place in a new open space: 'the unmapped spaces of the internet' (Zuboff, 2019, p. 9) or 'the world's largest ungoverned space'

(Schmidt & Cohen, 2014, p. 3). The construction of the Internet has taken place step by step without any player being able to predict what it would be. It started as a project within the US Armed Forces but was taken over in the 1980s by the National Science Foundation (NSF) in the USA, with the aim of developing it as a communication channel for researchers. In the early 1990s, management and development of the Internet was transferred to a number of other organizations and several of the meta-organizations mentioned in this chapter were formed. As Greenstein (2015), who researched the commercialization of the Internet, stated: 'Lack of a dominant firm in computing or communications would be crucial for the Internet's growth' (p. 38).[3] Two large, established companies in the USA that could have been considered for taking over the Internet were International Business Machines Corporation (IBM), founded in 1911; and American Telephone and Telegraph Company (AT&T), founded in 1885. IBM was active in this field in the 1980s but lost its leadership position due to its inertia or its 'inability to dominate any markets other than its traditional market, large-scale computing' (p. 37). According to Greenstein, the timing was wrong for AT&T. The company had been perceived by most people in the industry as a bureaucratic colossus, but by that time it had been weakened by being forced into a division through US antitrust laws (p. 83).

All the organizations that have become large and dominant on the Internet have been new companies such as Apple, Google, Facebook, Amazon, and Microsoft. What became Google began in a protected space at Stanford University funded by research grants from NSF (Greenstein, 2015, pp. 369–371). At the beginning, there was no thought of Google making money from advertisements or by selling data that described the people and organizations that use its search services. The sudden, major economic crisis in the industry around 2000 prompted the owners to rethink their business model, and they came up with a new way of making money from their existing business. This strategy has been described by Zuboff (2019) as an introduction to what can be called 'surveillance capitalism': 'Google had discovered a way to translate its nonmarket interactions with users into surplus raw material for the fabrication of products aimed at genuine market transactions with its real customers: advertisers' (p. 93). This new logic of accumulation spread to Facebook, among other companies, when Facebook recruited someone who was involved in the development of Google's business idea (p. 92).

The Internet turned out to be a new, open space with a rare dynamic. Things happened at a furious pace. For the original organizations, there was plenty of room to conquer. It was also a space that offered many surprises, and early plans and ambitions changed rapidly. It was not the case that the design of companies was determined by technology. The development of surveillance capitalism 'was invented by a specific group of human beings in a specific time and place. It is not an inherent result of digital technology, nor is it a necessary expression of information capitalism' (Zuboff, 2019, p. 85).

The existence of options demonstrates the development of Wikipedia. But neither was the organizational design of Wikipedia originally planned. Unlike Google and Facebook, what became Wikipedia was intended to be financed through advertising revenue. The first version of Wikipedia was more like a traditional encyclopaedia, with articles edited and written by experts. But this work went far too slowly. When, in 2001, the founder became aware of the free online software, WikiWikiWeb, which enabled people to write and post articles themselves, the encyclopaedia grew explosively. The special culture that existed online at that time was a prerequisite for Wikipedia's rapid growth. Another condition was the crisis in the industry that freed resources in the form of programmers who lost their jobs or had less work to do. Wikipedia became a social movement, and almost all work was done on a nonprofit basis. When it became known that there were still plans to fund Wikipedia with advertisements, it provoked such strong protests from those who had invested so much volunteer work in building the encyclopaedia that Wikipedia was organized as a nonprofit foundation (Lih, 2009).

The Interplay Between Old and New

There is no doubt that organizations like Google and Facebook came up with something new, and that they have changed the world around them. But the question is whether they have changed society, and if so, which society? Their businesses extend all over the world, and they are found in almost every country. Google and Facebook have helped to make the world more striped and have created increased opportunities for communication between individuals. They have changed the conditions for news media and social communication. But they have not had to engage in creative destruction to become as large as they are. On the contrary, in the business model they have developed, they interact and collaborate with many old organizations, while parasitizing on their content and receiving their revenues. They are giant intermediaries. They are similar to traditional companies in most respects; they are listed on the stock market, and they are trying to place their profits in states with favourable terms.

Facebook, Google, and other new digital companies are good illustrations of rapid change occurring simultaneously and in parallel with stagnation or slow change. Not everything changes at the same time; organizations and other relationships are changing at an uneven pace. By examining the demands made to stop global warming, we can see that most companies in the world are characterized by inertia and that changes are taking place slowly in defined paths, not least in the large oil companies and the food industry.

When organizations change at an uneven pace; when rapid changes occur in parallel with a standstill, it is not about system changes. In attempts to describe social conditions in different parts of the world today, the prefix 'post' is often used; society is post-something: postmodern, post-industrial, post-socialist, or post-colonial. But such labels say nothing about how it is – only what it is thought to have been. They testify to the difficulties of categorizing social conditions. New constellations of organizations are constantly emerging that do not fit into any models. In a book on contemporary Russian politics, Neil Robinson (2018) asks what kind of polity Russia represents. One way to address this issue is to talk about hybridity, but as Robinson also states: 'Russia can change more quickly than the labels used about it in the literature' (p. 246). In the fourth part of his extensive work on sources of social power, sociologist Michael Mann (2013) wrote that it is difficult to find a term that could summarize what China currently represents. He quotes with approval an author who describes China as 'a successful stir-fry of markets, socialism and traditional China that is fully none of the three … all tossed together over very high heat' (p. 231). His own proposal for a label is 'a capitalist party-state' (p. 234), which is a description of a new, unique combination of companies, the world's largest political party, and an old state.

Not everything changes at once. That would be impossible. We would not know where we were or what we would do. We would be completely lost. Change must be understood as a contrast, in relation to something else: How was it before the change and how was it in relation to its environment? In a world with an increasing number of global relationships, we must understand change in the interaction that occurs between old and new in various forms of collaboration, conflict, and competition. And it is not obvious that what is new points to the future. Old organizations can try to emulate new ones, but new organizations may eventually become more similar to existing ones. What is new or old is also not self-evident. Old and new are not merely about time; they are also about space. Old organizations can become 'new' in a new environment.

When new organizations are established in open spaces, there will be more organizations. Meta-organizations and temporary organizations as projects also lead to more organization. In addition, partial organization is created in various forms, such as standards or prizes and rankings. As Bromley and Meyer (2015) state in their book, *Hyper-Organization*, 'Faced with any problematic situations, the modern impulse is to create more organizational structures' (p. 4). With greater organization come more rules, more boundaries to cross, and more division between those who are included and those who are excluded. And with more organization, according to Simmel (1909, p. 303), more society arises, leading to a densification of the social landscape, in which the interaction between organizations is becoming increasingly important.

Organizations change slowly, mainly through rationalizations, which increase in step with digitalization; people are replaced by technology. Organizations become less dependent on people and more dependent on other organizations, resulting in more organization with fewer people. It can lead to a weakening of people's social bonds.

There is a tendency for more precarious and insecure employment relationships (Kalleberg, 2011): rental of employees to other companies and new forms of insecure social bonds to digital platforms such as Uber and Lyft. There are no permanent jobs in such companies, but digitalization enables tight monitoring (Kirchner & Schüßler, 2019). Migrant labour means temporary employment. Millions of refugees around the world live in countries where they have only temporary, if any, right to stay. Researchers say that globalization has given rise to a precariat, a large group of people around the world whose lives are marked by weak social bonds, no sense of secure occupational identity, and few if any entitlements to state and enterprise benefits (Standing, 2014, p. 4).

The diversity of the world has changed patterns; instead of squares, there are stripes. Different places in the world are characterized by greater diversity, but this diversity contains the same components, albeit in different proportions. This situation can apply to everything from religion to sports. Football has spread from England to large parts of the world, and martial arts from Asia has spread to Europe and North America. McDonald's has spread through franchising to many countries, even as many of the world's food cultures have spread through reverse globalization to many countries through migrants who have opened restaurants where they serve the cuisine of their home countries.

Many of the world's diverse cuisines have challenged the status of French cuisine as the world's leading haute cuisine. This change through proliferation has been triggered by a 'culinary intermediary': the World's 50 Best Restaurants (W50B) list, a ranking that covers a larger number of countries than previous rankings. It is based on a complicated voting procedure and has, like most decision-making processes, been criticized, but it has nevertheless gradually gained a great deal of legitimacy. Through this list, the culinary traditions of several countries, such as Peru, Chile, Thailand, and South Korea, have been recognized, with their new forms of haute cuisine. Several of the restaurants that have been on the list have established themselves in such major cities as London once recognized by The World's 50 Best Restaurants (Lane, 2019).

Although globalization leads to an interconnection of various parts of the world, many people's lifeworlds become more fragmented. Thus, a world with global compartments of relationships and changing social bonds must be understood from a relational perspective.

NOTES

1. One critique of the term 'globalization' is that it gives the impression of being about processes that literally extend all over the world. Rather, the argument goes, one should refer to processes that transcend national borders as 'transnational'. (See, for example, Djelic & Sahlin-Andersson, 2006; Hannerz, 1993.) There is a valid point to this criticism, yet it gives too much weight to the national. And I believe that one can use the term 'globalization', bearing in mind that it is not necessarily about relationships that extend across the whole globe.

2. In this respect, we see a difference between the idea of open spaces and the concept of niche, which is used especially in population ecology (cf. Aldrich, 1999; Hannan & Carroll, 1992). An open space is more indeterminate than a niche, which is seen more as fitted to certain kinds of organizations.

3. Greenstein uses the term 'innovation from the edges' to express a thought reminiscent of the emphasis on space:

    innovation from the edges describes innovation being commercialized by suppliers who lacked power in the old market structure, who the central firms regarded as peripheral participants in the supply of services, and who perceived economic opportunities outside of the prevailing view. This definition embeds three related interpretations – stressing place, power or perceptions. (2015, p. 11)

References

Abrahamsson, Bengt (2007), *Hierarki: Om ordning, makt och kristallisering*, Malmö: Liber.

Acker, Joan (2006), 'Inequality regimes: Gender, class, and race in organizations', *Gender & Society*, **20**(4), 441–464.

Ackroyd, Stephen (2002), *The Organization of Business: Applying Organizational Theory to Contemporary Change*, Oxford: Oxford University Press.

Ackroyd, Stephen, Gibson Burell, Michael Hughes & Alan Whitaker (2007a), 'The Japanization of British industry?', *Industrial Relations Journal*, **19**(1), 11–23.

Ackroyd, Stephen, Ian Kirkpatrick & Richard Walker (2007b), 'Public management reform in the UK and its consequences for professional organization: A comparative analysis', *Public Administration*, **85**(1), 9–26.

Adeniji, Anna (2008), *Inte den typ som gifter sig: Feministiska samtal om äktenskaps-motstånd*, Göteborg: Makadam förlag.

Ahrne, Göran (1981), *Vardagsverklighet och struktur*, Göteborg: Bokförlaget Korpen.

Ahrne, Göran (1990), *Agency and Organization*, London: SAGE.

Ahrne, Göran (1994), *Social Organizations: Interaction Inside, Outside and Between Organizations*, London: SAGE.

Ahrne, Göran (2014), *Samhället mellan oss: Om vänskap, kärlek, relationer och organ-isationer*, Stockholm: Liber.

Ahrne, Göran (2019), 'Organizing intimacy', in Göran Ahrne & Nils Brunsson (eds), *Organization outside Organizations: The Abundance of Partial Organization in Social Life*, Cambridge: Cambridge University Press, pp. 235–252.

Ahrne, Göran & Nils Brunsson (2004), 'Regler innanför och utanför organisationer', in Göran Ahrne & Nils Brunsson (eds), *Regelexplosionen*, Stockholm: EFI, pp. 45–60.

Ahrne, Göran & Nils Brunsson (2008), *Meta-Organizations*, Cheltenham, UK and Northampton, MA, USA: Edward Elgar Publishing.

Ahrne, Göran & Nils Brunsson (2011), 'Organization outside organizations: The signif-icance of partial organization', *Organization*, **18**(1), 83–104.

Ahrne, Göran & Nils Brunsson (2014), 'The travel of organization', in Gili S. Drori, Markus A. Höllerer & Peter Walgenbach (eds), *Global Themes and Local Variations in Organization and Management*, London: Routledge, pp. 39–51.

Ahrne, Göran & Nils Brunsson (2019), 'Organization unbound', in Göran Ahrne & Nils Brunsson (eds), *Organization outside Organizations: The Abundance of Partial Organization in Social Life*, Cambridge: Cambridge University Press, pp. 3–36.

Ahrne, Göran & Daniel Castillo (2020), 'The persistence of rock-groups', unpublished paper, Stockholm Centre for Organizational Research.

Ahrne, Göran & Christina Garsten (1998), 'Stat och företag som arbetsförmedlare', in Göran Ahrne (ed.), *Stater som organisationer*, Stockholm: Nerenius & Santérus Förlag, pp. 309–331.

Ahrne, Göran & Apostolis Papakostas (2014), *Organisationer, samhälle och glo-balisering*, Lund: Studentlitteratur.

Ahrne, Göran & Amir Rostami (2019), 'How is "organized crime" organized?', in Göran Ahrne & Nils Brunsson (eds), *Organization outside Organizations: The Abundance of Partial Organization in Social Life*, Cambridge: Cambridge University Press, pp. 253–270.

Ahrne, Göran & Adrienne Sörbom (2020), *Flawed Globalization: Why Traditional Political Organizations Have Problems Forming Transnational Meta-organizations*, Scores rapportserie 2020:3, Stockholm: Stockholm Centre for Organizational Research.

Ahrne, Göran, Patrik Aspers & Nils Brunsson (2018), 'The organization of markets', in Nils Brunsson & Mats Jutterström (eds), *Organizing & Reorganizing Markets*, Oxford: Oxford University Press, pp. 17–31.

Ahrne, Göran, Nils Brunsson & David Seidl (2016), 'Resurrecting organization by going beyond organizations', *European Management Journal*, **34**(2), 93–101.

Ahrne, Göran, Daniel Castillo & Lambros Roumbanis (2019), 'Queues: Tensions between institution and organization', in Göran Ahrne & Nils Brunsson (eds), *Organization outside Organizations: The Abundance of Partial Organization in Social Life*, Cambridge: Cambridge University Press, pp. 177–188.

Åkesson, Lisa (2011), 'Remittances and relationships: Exchange in Cape Verdean transnational families', *Ethnos*, **76**(3), 326–347.

Alberoni, Francesco (2016), *Friendship*, Leiden: Brill.

Albrow, Martin (1996), *The Global Age: State and Society beyond Modernity*, Cambridge: Polity Press.

Aldrich, Howard (1999), *Organizations Evolving*, London: SAGE.

Alexius, Susanna & Staffan Furusten (2019), 'Exploring constitutional hybridity', in Susanna Alexius & Staffan Furusten (eds), *Managing Hybrid Organizations: Governance, Professionalism and Regulation*, Basingstoke: Palgrave Macmillan, pp. 1–25.

Alvesson, Mats (2015), *Organisationskultur och ledning*, 3:e upplagan, Stockholm: Norstedts Juridik.

Arnold, Jason Ross (2020), *Whistleblowers, Leakers, and Their Networks: From Snowden to Samizdat*, London: Rowman & Littlefield.

Arora-Jonsson, Stefan, Nils Brunsson & Raimund Hasse (2020), 'Where does competition come from? The role of organization', *Organization Theory*, **1**(1), 1–24.

Arora-Jonsson, Stefan, Nils Brunsson & Raimund Hasse (2021a), 'A new understanding of competition', in Stefan Arora-Jonsson, Nils Brunsson, Raimund Hasse & Katarina Lagerström (eds), *Competition: What It Is and Why It Happens*, Oxford: Oxford University Press, pp. 1–25.

Arora-Jonsson, Stefan, Nils Brunsson, Raimund Hasse & Katarina Lagerström (2021b), 'Competition unbundled: Taking stock and looking forward', in Stefan Arora-Jonsson, Nils Brunsson, Raimund Hasse & Katarina Lagerström (eds), *Competition: What It Is and Why It Happens*, Oxford: Oxford University Press, chapter 14.

Azarian, Reza (2010), 'Social ties: Elements of a substantive conceptualization', *Acta Sociologica*, **53**(4), 323–338.

Badgett, M. V. Lee (2009), *When Gay People Get Married: What Happens When Societies Legalize Same-Sex Marriage*, New York: New York University Press.

Barbero, José, José C. Casillas, Mike Wright & Alicia Ramos Garcia (2014), 'Do different types of incubators produce different types of innovations?', *Journal of Technological Transfer*, **39**(2), 151–168.

Barbot, Cristina (2006), 'Low-cost airlines, secondary airports, and state aid: An economic assessment of the Ryanair-Charleroi Airport agreement', *Journal of Air Transport Management*, **12**, 197–203.

Barkman, Tobias & Joakim Palmkvist (2011), *Maffiakrig*, Stockholm: Albert Bonniers Förlag.

Barnard, Chester (1968), *The Functions of the Executive*, 30th anniversary edition, Cambridge, MA: Harvard University Press.

Baubäck, Rainer (2019), 'Genuine links and useful passports: Evaluating strategic uses of citizenship', *Journal of Ethnic and Migration Studies*, **45**(6), 1015–1026.

Bento da Silva, Jose & Ioanna Iordanou (2018), 'The origins of organizing in the sixteenth century', in Tuomo Peltonen, Hugo Gaggiotti & Peter Case (eds), *Origins of Organizing*, Cheltenham, UK and Northampton, MA, USA: Edward Elgar Publishing, pp. 129–146.

Berger, Peter & Thomas Luckmann (1991), *The Social Construction of Reality: A Treatise in the Sociology of Knowledge*, Harmondsworth: Penguin Books.

Bergman Blix, Stina (2010), 'Rehearsing emotions: The process of creating a role for the stage', Dissertation, Stockholm: Stockholm University.

Bergman Blix, Stina (2015), 'Professional emotion management as a rehearsal process', *Professions & Professionalism*, **5**(2), 1–15.

Bergman Blix, Stina & Åsa Wettergren (2018), *Professional Emotions in Court: A Sociological Perspective*, Abingdon: Routledge.

Berkowitz, Héloïse & Sanne Bor (2019), 'The partial organization of meta-organizations', Paper for the 1st Toulouse Workshop Meta- Macro- and Partial Organization.

Berkowitz, Héloïse & Hervé Dumez (2015), 'La dynamique des dispositifs d'action collective entre firmes: le cas des métaorganisations dans le secteur pétrolier', *L'Anné Sociologique*, **65**(2), 333–356.

Besio, Cristina, Paul du Gay & Kathia Serrano Velarde (2020), 'Disappearing organization? Reshaping the sociology of organizations', *Current Sociology Monograph*, **68**(4), 411–418.

Blinder, Alan (2009), 'How many US jobs might be offshoreable?', *World Economics*, **10**(2), 41–78.

Boas, Max & Steve Chain (1976), *Big Mac: The Unauthorized Story of McDonald's*, New York: New American Library.

Bommes, Michael & Veronika Tacke (2005), 'Luhmann's systems theory and network theory', in David Seidl & Kai Helge Becker (eds), *Niklas Luhmann and Organization Studies*, Malmö: Liber, pp. 282–304.

Borgatti, Stephen P. & Pacey Foster (2003), 'The network paradigm in organizational research: A review and typology', *Journal of Management*, **29**(6), 991–1013.

Borgatti, Stephen P. & Daniel S. Halgin (2011), 'On network theory', *Organization Science*, **22**(5), 1168–1181.

Braudel, Fernand (1982), *The Wheels of Commerce*, London: William Collins.

Bromley, Patricia & John Meyer (2015), *Hyper-Organization: Global Organizational Expansion*, Oxford: Oxford University Press.

Brunsson, Nils (2006), *Mechanisms of Hope: Maintaining the Dream of the Rational Organization*, Malmö: Liber AB.

Brunsson, Nils (2007), *The Consequences of Decision-Making*, Oxford: Oxford University Press.

Brunsson, Nils (2020), 'Institution und organisation: Zur Gegenüberstellung von zwei Schlüsselkonzepten', in Raimund Hasse & Anne K. Krüger (eds),

Neo-Institutionalismus: Kritik und Weiterentwicklung eines sozialwissenschaftliches Forschungsprograms, Bielefeld: Transcript Verlag, pp. 51–71.

Brunsson, Nils & Mats Jutterström (eds) (2018), *Organizing & Reorganizing Markets*, Oxford: Oxford University Press.

Burns, Tom (1992), *Erving Goffman*, London: Routledge.

Burns, Tom & George M. Stalker (1961), *The Management of Innovation*, London: Tavistock.

Burt, Ronald S. (2005), *Brokerage and Closure: An Introduction to Social Capital*, Oxford: Oxford University Press.

Callaghan, George & Paul Thompson (2001), 'Edwards revisited: Technical control and call centres', *Economic and Industrial Democracy*, **22**(1), 13–37.

Carey, Matthew (2017), *Mistrust: An Ethnographic Theory*, Chicago, IL: HAU Books.

Carsten, Janet (2000), 'Introduction: Cultures of relatedness', in Janet Carsten (ed.), *Cultures of Relatedness: New Approaches to the Study of Kinship*, Cambridge: Cambridge University Press, pp. 1–36.

Castillo, Daniel (2013), *Farliga förbindelser? Statens förändrade gränser och näringslivets nya möjligheter*, Stockholm School of Economics Institute for Research.

Catino, Maurizio (2019), *Mafia Organizations: The Visible Hand of Criminal Enterprise*, Cambridge: Cambridge University Press.

Chandler, Alfred Dupont (1962), *Strategy and Structure: Chapters in the History of Industrial Enterprise*, Cambridge, MA: MIT Press.

Chartrand, Sébastien (2004), 'Work in voluntary welfare organizations: A sociological study of voluntary welfare organizations in Sweden', Dissertation, Stockholm University.

Chauncey, George (2004), *Why Marriage? The History Shaping Today's Debate Over Gay Equality*, New York: Basic Books.

Christensen, Tom & Per Lægreid (eds) (2001), *New Public Management: The Transformation of Ideas and Practice*, Aldershot: Ashgate.

Clark, Duncan (2016), *Alibaba: The House that Jack Ma Built*, New York: Ecco Harper Collins.

Clegg, Stewart (1989), *Frameworks of Power*, London: SAGE.

Cleland, Jamie, Mark Doidge, Peter Millward & Paul Widdop (eds) (2018), *Collective Action and Football Fandom: A Relational Sociological Approach*, London: Palgrave Macmillan.

Cockburn, Cynthia (1991), *In the Way of Women: Men's Resistance to Sex Equality in Organizations*, London: Macmillan.

Coleman, James (1990), *Foundations of Social Theory*, Cambridge, MA: Belknap Press of Harvard University Press.

Collins, Randall (1981), 'On the microfoundations of macrosociology', *American Journal of Sociology*, **86**(3), 984–1014.

Cooley, Charles Horton (1909), *Social Organization: A Study of the Larger Mind*, New York: Scribner.

Coser, Lewis A. (1964), 'The political function of eunuchism', *American Sociological Review*, **29**(6), 880–885.

Coser, Lewis A. (1967), 'Greedy organizations', *Archives Européennes de Sociologie*, **7**(2), 196–215.

Crossley, Nick (2011), *Towards Relational Sociology*, London: Routledge.

Crossley, Nick (2015), 'Relational sociology and culture: A preliminary framework', *International Review of Sociology*, **25**(1), 65–85.

Crozier, Michel (1964), *The Bureaucratic Phenomenon*, Chicago, IL: University of Chicago Press.

Cyert, Richard M. & James March (1992), *A Behavioral Theory of the Firm*, 2nd edition, Cambridge, MA: Blackwell.

Czarniawska, Barbara (2009), 'Emerging institutions: Pyramids or anthills?', *Organization Studies*, **30**(4), 423–441.

Czarniawska, Barbara & Guje Sevón (2005), 'Translation is a vehicle, imitation its motor and fashion sits at the wheel', in Barbara Czarniawska & Guje Sevón (eds), *Global Ideas: How Ideas, Objects and Practices Travel in the Global Economy*, Malmö: Liber & Copenhagen Business School Press, pp. 7–12.

Czarniawska, Barbara & Roland Solli (2016), 'Hybridisering av offentliga organisationer', *Nordiske Organisasjonsstudier*, **18**(2), 23–36.

Czarniawska-Joerges, Barbara & Bernward Joerges (1996), 'Travels of ideas', in Barbara Czarniawska-Joerges & Guje Sevón (eds), *Translating Organizational Change*, Berlin: de Gruyter, pp. 13–48.

Davis, Gerald F. (2016), *The Vanishing American Corporation: Navigating the Hazards of a New Economy*, Oakland, CA: Berrett-Koehler Publishers.

Decker, Scott H. & David C. Pyrooz (2015), *The Handbook of Gangs*, New York: John Wiley & Sons.

den Hond, Frank, Frank G. A. de Bakker & Nikolai Smith (2015), 'Social movements and organizational analysis', in Donatella Della Porta & Mario Diani (eds), *The Oxford Handbook of Social Movements*, Oxford: Oxford University Press, pp. 291–305.

Dépelteau, Francois (2008), 'Relational thinking: A critique of co-deterministic theories of structure and agency', *Sociological Theory*, **26**(1), 51–73.

Dietschy, Paul (2013), 'Making football global? FIFA, Europe, and the non-European football world 1912–74', *Journal of Global History*, **8**(2), 279–298.

DiMaggio, Paul (2001), 'Conclusion: The futures of business organization and paradoxes of change', in Paul DiMaggio (ed.), *The Twenty-first-century Firm: Changing Economic Organization in International Perspective*, Princeton, NJ: Princeton University Press, pp. 210–243.

Djelic, Marie-Laure (2014), 'Competition regulation in Africa between global and local: A banyan tree story', in Gili S. Drori, Markus A. Höllerer & Peter Walgenbach (eds), *Global Themes and Local Variations in Organization and Management*, London: Routledge, pp. 90–103.

Djelic, Marie-Laure & Kerstin Sahlin-Andersson (2006), 'Introduction: A world of governance: The rise of transnational regulation', in Marie-Laure Djelic & Kerstin Sahlin-Andersson (eds), *Transnational Governance: Institutional Dynamics of Regulation*, Cambridge: Cambridge University Press, pp. 1–28.

Donati, Pierpaolo (2011), *Relational Sociology: A New Paradigm for the Social Sciences*, London: Routledge.

Du Gay, Paul & Signe Vikkelsø (2012), 'Reflections on the lost specification of "change"', *Journal of Change Management*, **12**(2), 121–143.

Dumez, Hervé & Sandra Renou (2020), *How Business Organizes Collectively: An Inquiry on Trade Associations and Other Meta-organizations*, Cheltenham, UK and Northampton, MA, USA: Edward Elgar Publishing.

Edlund, Peter, Josef Pallas & Linda Wedlin (2019), "Prizes and the organization of status", in Göraan Ahrne & NilsBrunsson (eds), *Organization outside Organizations. The Abundance of Partial Organization in Social Life*, Cambridge: Cambridge University Press, pp. 62-83.

Edwards, Richard C. (1979), *Contested Terrain: The Transformation of the Workplace in the Twentieth Century*, New York: Basic Books.

Eley, Geoff (2002), *Forging Democracy: The History of the Left in Europe, 1850–2000*, Oxford: Oxford University Press.

Elger, Tony & Chris Smith (1994), 'Global Japanization? Convergence and competition in the organization of the labour process', in Tony Elger & Chris Smith (eds), *Global Japanization? The Transnational Transformation of the Labour Process*, London: Routledge, pp. 31–59.

Elias, Norbert (1978), *What is Sociology?*, London: Hutchinson.

Elias, Norbert & John L. Scotson (1994), *The Established and the Outsiders*, 2nd edition, London: SAGE.

Emerson, Richard (1962), 'Power-dependence relations', *American Sociological Review*, 27(1), 31–41.

Emirbayer, Mustafa (1997), 'Manifesto for a relational sociology', *American Journal of Sociology*, 103(2), 281–317.

Etzioni, Amitai (1961), *A Comparative Analysis of Complex Organizations: On Power, Involvement and their Correlates*, New York: Free Press.

Etzioni, Amitai (1968), *The Active Society: A Theory of Societal and Political Processes*, New York: Free Press.

Farrell, Michael P. (2001), *Collaborative Circles: Friendship Dynamics and Creative Work*, Chicago, IL: University of Chicago Press.

Finch, Janet (1989), *Family Obligations and Social Change*, Cambridge: Polity Press.

Fligstein, Neil & Doug McAdam (2012), *A Theory of Fields*, Oxford: Oxford University Press.

Forssell, Anders & Anders Ivarsson Westerberg (2014), *Administrationssamhället*, Lund: Studentlitteratur.

Forstorp, Per-Anders & Ulf Mellström (2018), *Higher Education, Globalization and Eduscapes: Towards a Critical Anthropology of a Global Knowledge Society*, London: Palgrave Macmillan.

Foucault, Michel (1979), *Discipline and Punish: The Birth of the Prison*, Harmondsworth: Penguin.

Freeman, Jo (1972), 'The tyranny of structurelessness', *Berkeley Journal of Sociology*, 17, 151–164.

Friedland, Roger, John, W. Mohr, Henk Roose & Paolo Gardinali (2014), 'The institutional logic of love: Measuring intimate life', *Theory and Society*, 43(3/4), 333–370.

Frisby, David & Derek Sayer (1986), *Society*, London: Tavistock Publications.

Fuhse, Jan (2015), 'Theorizing social networks: The relational sociology of and around Harrison White', *International Review of Sociology*, 25(1), 15–44.

Fukuyama, Francis (2012), *The Origins of Political Order: From Prehuman Times to the French Revolution*, New York: Farrar, Straus and Giroux.

Fukuyama, Francis (2015), *Political Order and Political Decay: From the Industrial Revolution to the Globalization of Democracy*, London: Profile Books.

Garfield, Alan E. (1997), 'Promises of silence: Contract law and freedom of speech', *Cornell Law Review*, 88, 261–364.

Garsten, Christina & Adrienne Sörbom (2018), *Discrete Power: How the World Economic Forum Shapes Market Agendas*, Stanford, CA: Stanford University Press.

Gereffi, Gary & Karina Fernandez-Stark (2011), *Global Value Chain Analysis: A Primer*, Center on globalization, governance & competitiveness, Duke University, North Carolina.

Giddens, Anthony (1984), *The Constitution of Society: Outline of the Theory of Structuration*, Cambridge: Polity Press.

Giddens, Anthony (1990), *Consequences of Modernity*, Cambridge: Polity Press.

Giulianotti, Richard & Roland Robertson (2009), *Globalization & Football*, London: SAGE.

Goffman, Erving (1959), *The Presentation of Self in Everyday Life*, New York: Double Day Anchor Books.

Goffman, Erving (1961), *Encounters: Two Studies in the Sociology of Interaction*, Harmondsworth: Penguin University Books.

Goffman, Erving (1968), *Asylums: Essays on the Social Situation of Mental Patients and Other Inmates*, Harmondsworth: Penguin Books.

Goffman, Erving (1971), *Relations in Public: Microstudies of the Public Order*, New York: Harper & Row.

Gouldner, Alvin (1959), *For Sociology: Renewal and Critique in Sociology Today*, Harmondsworth: Penguin Books.

Granovetter, Mark (1973), 'The strength of weak ties', *American Journal of Sociology*, **78**(6), 1360–1380.

Greenstein, Shane (2015), *How the Internet Became Commercial: Innovation, Privatization and the Birth of a New Network*, Princeton, NJ: Princeton University Press.

Grosser, Travis, Virginie Lopez-Kidwell & Giuseppe Labianca (2010), 'A social network analysis of positive and negative gossip in organizational life', *Group & Organization Management*, **35**(2), 177–212.

Grothe-Hammer, Michael (2019), 'Membership or contributorship? Managing the inclusion of individuals into organizations', in Göran Ahrne & Nils Brunsson (eds), *Organization outside Organizations: The Abundance of Partial Organization in Social Life*, Cambridge: Cambridge University Press, pp. 84–111.

Habermas, Jürgen (1981), *Theorie des Kommunikativen Handelns. Band 2. Zur Kritik der Funktionalistischen Vernunft*, Frankfurt am Main: Suhrkamp Verlag.

Haglunds, Magnus (2009), 'Enemies of the people: Whistle-blowing and the sociology of tragedy', Dissertation, Stockholm University.

Hall, Patrik, Vesa Leppänen & Malin Åkerström (2019), *Mötesboken: Tolkningar av arbetslivets sammanträden och rosémingel*, Malmö: Egalité.

Hall, Peter (1998), *Cities in Civilization*, London: Weidenfeld & Nicolson.

Hall, Richard (2010), 'Renewing and revising the engagement between labour process theory and technology', in Paul Thompson & Chris Smith (eds), *Working Life: Renewing Labour Process Analysis*, Basingstoke: Palgrave Macmillan, pp. 157–181.

Hannan, Michael & Glenn Carroll (1992), *Dynamics of Organizational Populations: Density, Legitimation, and Competition*, New York: Oxford University Press.

Hannan, Michael & John Freeman (1989), *Organizational Ecology*, Cambridge, MA: Harvard University Press.

Hannerz, Ulf (1993), *Cultural Complexity: Studies in the Social Organization of Meaning*, New York: Columbia University Press.

Hardin, Russel (1982), *Collective Action*, Baltimore, MD: Johns Hopkins University Press.

Heater, Derek (1999), *What is Citizenship?*, Cambridge: Polity Press.

Hechter, Michael (1987), *Principles of Group Solidarity*, Berkeley: University of California Press.

Heydebrand, Wolf (1989), 'New organizational forms', *Work and Occupations*, **16**(3), 323–357.

Hirschi, Travis (1969), *Causes of Delinquency*, Berkeley: University of California Press.

Hirschman, Albert O. (1970), *Exit, Voice, and Loyalty: Responses to Decline in Firms, Organizations, and States*, Cambridge, MA: Harvard University Press.

Hjort, Katrin (2007), 'Epilogue: What's new, Doc?', in Carola Aili, Lars-Erik Nilsson, Lennart Svensson & Pamela Denicolo (eds), *In Tension between Organization and Profession*, Lund: Nordic Academic Press, pp. 322–330.

Hochschild, Arlie Russell (1983), *The Managed Heart – Commercialization of Human Feeling*, Berkeley: University of California Press.

Homans, George Caspar (1951), *The Human Group*, London: Routledge & Kegan Paul.

Huzell, Henrietta (2015), 'Utseendekrav i arbetet', in Ann Bergman, Gunnar Gillberg & Lars Ivarsson (eds), *Tankar om arbete*, Stockholm: Premiss Förlag, pp. 176–196.

Iannacone, Laurence R. (1994), 'Why strict churches are strong', *American Journal of Sociology*, **99**(5), 1180–1211.

Ingram, Paul (1998), 'Changing the rules: Interest, organizations, and institutional change in the US hospitality industry', in Mary C. Brinton & Victor Nee (eds), *The New Institutionalism in Sociology*, New York: Russell Sage Foundation, pp. 258–276.

James, Paul (2006), *Globalism, Nationalism, Tribalism: Bringing Theory Back In*, London: SAGE.

Jepperson, Ronald L. (1991), 'Institutions, institutional effects, and institutionalism', in Walter Powell & Paul DiMaggio (eds), *The New Institutionalism in Organizational Analysis*, Chicago, IL: Chicago University Press, pp. 143–163.

Joas, Hans (1996), *The Creativity of Action*, Cambridge: Polity Press.

Joas, Hans (2003), *War and Modernity*, Cambridge: Polity Press.

Joas, Hans & Wolfgang Knöbl (2009), *Social Theory: Twenty Introductory Lectures*, Cambridge: Cambridge University Press.

Johansson, Göran (1992), 'More blessed to give: A Pentecostal mission to Bolivia in anthropological perspective', Dissertation, Stockholm University.

Jones, Geoffrey (2005), *Renewing Unilever: Transformation and Tradition*, Oxford: Oxford University Press.

Kalleberg, Arne (2011), *Good Jobs, Bad Jobs: The Rise of Polarized and Precarious Employment Systems in the United States, 1970s to 2000s*, New York: Russell Sage Foundation.

Kalleberg, Arne & Peter Marsden (2005), 'Externalizing organizational activities: Where and how U.S. establishments use employment intermediaries', *Socioeconomic Review*, **3**(3), 389–416.

Kanter, Rosabeth Moss & Robert G. Eccles (1992), 'Conclusion: Making network research relevant to practice', in Nitin Nohria & Robert G. Eccles (eds), *Networks and Organizations: Structure, Form and Action*, Boston, MA: Harvard Business School Press, pp. 521–527.

Karlsson, Jan Ch., Egil J. Skorstad & Jonas Axelsson (2015), 'On the track of the worker collectivity: Its various adventures over the past 60 years', *Journal of Workplace Rights*, April–June, 1–13.

Kaufman, Herbert (1995), *The Limits of Organizational Change*, with a new introduction by the author, Piscataway, NJ: Transaction Publishers.

Kemper, Theodore D. (2012), *Status, Power, and Ritual Interaction: A Relational Reading of Durkheim, Goffman and Collins*, Farnham: Ashgate.

Kirchner, Stefan & Elke Schüßler (2019), 'The organization of digital marketplaces: Unmasking the role of Internet platforms in the sharing economy', in Göran Ahrne &

Nils Brunsson (eds), *Organization outside Organizations: The Abundance of Partial Organization in Social Life*, Cambridge: Cambridge University Press, pp. 131–154.

Klein, Malcolm (2016), *Chasing after Street Gangs*, Oxford: Oxford University Press.

Kolb, Kenneth H. (2011), 'Sympathy work: Identity and emotion management among victim-advocates and counselors', *Qualitative Sociology*, **34**(1), 101–119.

Korpi, Walter (1985), 'Power resources approach vs. action and conflict: On causal and intentional explanations in the study of power', *Sociological Theory*, **3**(2), 31–45.

Laamanen, Mikko, Sanne Bor & Frank den Hond (2019), 'The dilemma of organization in social movement initiatives', in Göran Ahrne & Nils Brunsson (eds), *Organization Unbound: The Abundance of Partial Organization in Social Life*, Cambridge: Cambridge University Press, pp. 293–317.

Lane, Christel (2019), 'Reverse cultural globalization: The case of haute cuisine in one global city', *Poetics*, **75**, 101350.

Lane, Christel & Geoffrey Wood (2009), 'Capitalist diversity and diversity within capitalism', *Economy and Society*, **38**(4), 531–551.

Lauchs, Mark, Andy Bain & Peter Bell (2015), *Outlaw Motorcycle Gangs: A Theoretical Perspective*, Basingstoke: Palgrave Macmillan.

Lawrence, Paul R. (1993), 'The contingency approach to organization design', in Robert T. Golembiewski (ed.), *Handbook of Organizational Behavior*, New York: Marcel Dekker, pp. 9–18.

Lawrence, Paul R. & Jay William Lorsch (1967), *Organization and Environment: Managing Differentiation and Integration*, Boston, MA: Graduate School of Business Administration, Harvard University.

Layder, Derek (2004), *Emotion in Social Life: The Lost Heart of Society*, London: SAGE.

Lewis, Jane (2001), *The End of Marriage? Individualism and Intimate Relations*, Cheltenham, UK and Northampton, MA, USA: Edward Elgar Publishing.

Lih, Andrew (2009), *The Wikipedia Revolution: How a Bunch of Nobodies Created the World's Greatest Encyclopedia*, New York: Hyperion.

Lillie, Nathan, Ines Wagner & Lise Bernsten (2014), 'Posted migration, spaces of exception, and the politics of labour relations in the European construction industry', in Marco Hauptmeier & Matti Vidal (eds), *Comparative Political Economy of Work*, Basingstoke: Palgrave Macmillan, pp. 312–331.

Lincoln, James & Arne Kalleberg (1990), *Culture, Control and Commitment: A Study of Work Organization and Work Attitudes in the United States and Japan*, Cambridge: Cambridge University Press.

Lindblom, Charles (1977), *Politics and Markets: The World's Political Economic Systems*, New York: Basic Books.

Littler, Craig (1982), *The Development of the Labour Process in Capitalist Societies*, London: Heinemann Educational Books.

Lizardo, Omar (2010), 'Beyond the antinomies of structure: Levi-Strauss, Giddens, Bourdieu, and Sewell', *Theory and Society*, **39**(6), 651–688.

Lizardo, Omar & Melissa Fletcher Pirkey (2014), 'How organizational theory can help network theorizing: Linking structure and dynamics via cross-level analogies', *Contemporary Perspectives on Organizational Social Networks: Research in the Sociology of Organizations*, **40**, 33–56.

Lonkila, Markku (2011), *Networks in the Russian Market Economy*, Basingstoke: Palgrave Macmillan.

Luhmann, Niklas (1986), *Love as Passion: The Codification of Intimacy*, Cambridge: Polity Press.

Luhmann, Niklas (1997), *Trust and Power*, Chichester: John Wiley.

Luhmann, Niklas (2018), *Organization and Decision*, Cambridge: Cambridge University Press.

Lukes, Stephen (1974), *Power: A Radical View*, London: Macmillan Press.

McEvily, Bill, Vincenzo Perrone & Akbar Zaheer (2003), 'Trust as an organizing principle', *Organization Science*, **14**(1), 91–103.

Mann, Michael (1986), *The Sources of Social Power. Volume 1: A History of Power from the Beginning to A.D. 1760*, Cambridge: Cambridge University Press.

Mann, Michael (2013), *The Sources of Social Power. Volume 4: Globalizations 1845–2011*, Cambridge: Cambridge University Press.

March, James (1991), 'Exploration and exploitation in organizational learning', *Organization Science*, **2**(1), 71–87.

March, James & Herbert Simon (1958), *Organizations*, New York: John Wiley.

March, James, Martin Schulz & Xueguang Zhou (2000), *The Dynamics of Rules: Change in Written Organizational Codes*, Stanford, CA: Stanford University Press.

Marglin, Stephen (1974), 'What do bosses do? The origins and functions of hierarchy in capitalist production', *The Review of Radical Political Economics*, **6**(2), 60–112.

Markovits, Andrei (1988), 'The other American exceptionalism – why is there no soccer in the United States?', *Praxis International*, **8**(2), 125–150.

Marshall, Gordon (1990), *In Praise of Sociology*, London: Unwin Hyman.

Martin, John Levi (2009), *Social Structures*, Princeton, NJ: Princeton University Press.

Mauss, Marcel (2002), *The Gift: The Form and Reason for Exchange in Archaic Societies*, London: Routledge.

Mazzucato, Mariana (2014), *The Entrepreneurial State: Debunking Public vs. Private Sector Myths*, London: Anthem Press.

Mechanic, David (1962), 'Sources of power of lower participants in complex organizations', *Administrative Science Quarterly*, **7**(3), 349–364.

Meyer, John & Brian Rowan (1977), 'Institutionalized organizations: Formal structure as myth and ceremony', *American Journal of Sociology*, **83**(2), 340–363.

Meyer, Marshall & Lynne Zucker (1989), *Permanently Failing Organizations*, Newbury Park, CA: SAGE.

Michels, Robert (1962), *Political Parties*, New York: Free Press.

Mills, C. Wright (1951), *White Collar: The American Middle Classes*, Oxford: Oxford University Press.

Mintzberg, Henry (1979), *The Structuring of Organizations: A Synthesis of the Research*, Englewood Cliffs, NJ: Prentice Hall.

Mintzberg, Henry (1993), *Structure in Fives: Designing Effective Organizations*, Upper Saddle River, NJ: Prentice Hall.

Mische, Ann (2011), 'Relational sociology, culture and agency', in John Scott & Peter J. Carrington (eds), *The SAGE Handbook of Social Network Analysis*, London: SAGE, pp. 80–97.

Mische, Ann & Harrison White (1998), 'Between conversation and situation: Public switching dynamics across network domains', *Social Research*, **65**(3), 695–724.

Morgan, Glenn, Peer Hull Kristensen & Richard Whitley (eds) (2001), *The Multinational Firm: Organizing Across Institutional and National Divides*, Oxford: Oxford University Press.

Mulinari, Paula (2007), 'Maktens fantasier & servicearbetets praktik: arbetsvillkor inom hotell- och restaurangbranschen i Malmö', Dissertation, Linköping University.

North, Douglass C. (1993), 'Institutions and credible commitment', *Journal of Institutional and Theoretical Economics*, **149**(1), 11–23.

North, Douglass C. (1998), 'Where have we been and where are we going?', in Avner Ben-Ner & Louis Putterman (eds), *Economics, Values and Organization*, Cambridge: Cambridge University Press, pp. 491–508.

Ostrom, Elinor (1990), *Governing the Commons: The Evolution of Institutions for Collective Action*, Cambridge: Cambridge University Press.

Outhwaite, William (2006), *The Future of Society*, Oxford: Blackwell Publishing.

Palan, Ronen, Richard Murphy & Christian Chavagneux (2010), *Tax Havens: How Globalization Really Works*, Ithaca, NY: Cornell University Press.

Papakostas, Apostolis (2012), *Civilizing the Public Sphere: Distrust, Trust and Corruption*, Basingstoke: Palgrave Macmillan.

Papakostas, Apostolis (2018), 'Building state infrastructural capacities: Sweden and Greece', in Fredrik Engelstad & Haldor Byrkjeflot (eds), *Bureaucracy and Society in Transition: Comparative Perspectives*, Bingley: Emerald Publishing, pp. 39–67.

Parsons, Talcott (1951), *The Social System*, Glencoe, IL: Routledge & Kegan Paul.

Parsons, Talcott (1966), *Societies: Evolutionary and Comparative Perspectives*, Englewood Cliffs, NJ: Prentice Hall.

Perrow, Charles (1984), *Normal Accidents: Living with High-Risk Technologies*, New York: Basic Books.

Perrow, Charles (1986), *Complex Organizations: A Critical Essay*, 3rd edition, New York: McGraw-Hill.

Perrow, Charles (2002), *Organizing America: Wealth, Power and the Origins of Corporate Capitalism*, Princeton, NJ: Princeton University Press.

Perrow, Charles (2007), *The Next Catastrophe: Reducing Our Vulnerabilities to Natural, Industrial, and Terrorist Disasters*, Princeton, NJ: Princeton University Press.

Pfeffer, Jeffrey (1981), *Power in Organizations*, Boston, MA: Pitman.

Pierson, Paul (2000), 'Increasing returns, path dependence, and the study of politics', *American Political Science Review*, **94**(2), 251–267.

Podolny, Joel M. & Karen L. Page (1998), 'Network forms of organization', *Annual Review of Sociology*, **24**, 57–76.

Powell, Walter (1990), 'Neither market nor hierarchy: Network forms of organization', in Larry L. Cummings & Barry M. Staw (eds), *Research in Organizational Behavior*, Greenwich, CT: JAI Press, pp. 295–336.

Power, Michael (1997), *The Audit Society: Rituals of Verification*, Oxford: Oxford University Press.

Prandini, Riccardo (2015), 'Relational sociology: A well-defined sociological paradigm or a challenging "relational turn" in sociology?', *International Review of Sociology*, **25**(1), 1–14.

Prowse, Catherine Elaine (2013), *Defining Street Gangs in the 21st Century: Fluid, Mobile, and Transnational Networks*, New York: Springer.

Rajan, Raghuram & Julie Wulf (2006), 'The flattening firm: Evidence from panel data on the changing nature of corporate hierarchies', *The Review of Economics and Statistics*, **88**(4), 759–773.

Robertson, Foster (1991), *Beyond the Family: The Social Organization of Human Reproduction*, Cambridge: Polity Press.

Robertson, Roland (1992), *Globalization: Social Theory and Global Culture*, London: SAGE.

Robertson, Roland (2014), 'Situating glocalization: A relatively autobiographical intervention', in Gili S. Drori, Markus A. Höllerer & Peter Walgenbach (eds),

Global Themes and Local Variations in Organization and Management, London: Routledge, pp. 25–36.

Robinson, Neil (2018), *Contemporary Russian Politics*, Cambridge: Polity Press.

Rosado-Serrano, Alexander, Paul Justin & Desislava Dikova (2018), 'International franchising: A literature review and research agenda', *Journal of Business Research* **85**, 238–257.

Rostami, Amir (2016), 'Policing gangs and organized crime: Reflections on conceptual confusion and its consequences from two Swedish case studies', in Cheryl L. Maxson & Finn-Aage Esbensen (eds), *Gang Transitions and Transformations in an International Context*, New York: Springer, pp. 279–289.

Rostami, Amir, Hernan Mondani, Fredrik Liljeros & Christoffer Edling (2018), 'Criminal organizing applying the theory of partial organization to four cases of organized crime', *Trends in Organized Crime*, **21**(4), 315–342.

Rotberg, Robert (ed.) (2004), *When States Fail: Causes and Consequences*, Princeton, NJ: Princeton University Press.

Rothman, Barbara Katz (2000), *Recreating Motherhood*, New Brunswick, NJ: Rutgers University Press.

Sandler, Jen & Renita Thedvall (2017), 'Introduction: Exploring the boring – an introduction to meeting ethnography', in Jen Sandler & Renita Thedvall (eds), *Meeting Ethnography: Meetings as Key Technologies of Contemporary Governance, Development, and Resistance*, London: Routledge, pp. 1–23.

Sarfatti-Larson, Magali (1979), *The Rise of Professionalism: A Sociological Analysis*, Berkeley: University of California Press.

Sartre, Jean-Paul (1976), *Critique of Dialectical Reason*, London: New Left Books.

Sassen, Saskia (2006), *Territory, Authority, Rights: From Medieval to Global Assemblages*, Princeton, NJ: Princeton University Press.

Scheff, Thomas (2006), *Goffman Unbound: A New Paradigm for Social Science*, Boulder, CO: Paradigm Publishers.

Schein, Edgar (1983), 'The role of the founder in creating organizational culture', *Organizational Dynamics*, **12**(1), 13–28.

Schmidt, Eric & Jared Cohen (2014), *The New Digital Age: Transforming Nations, Businesses and Our Lives*, New York: Vintage.

Schoeneborn, Dennis & Leonhard Dobusch (2019), 'Alternating between partial and complete organization: The case of anonymous', in Göran Ahrne & Nils Brunsson (eds), *Organization Unbound: The Abundance of Partial Organization in Social Life*, Cambridge: Cambridge University Press, pp. 318–333.

Schoeneborn, Dennis, Steffen Blaschke, Francois Cooren, Robert D. McPhee, David Seidl & James R. Taylor (2014), 'The three schools of CCO thinking: Interactive dialogue and systematic comparison', *Management Communication Quarterly*, **28**(2), 285–316.

Schumpeter, Joseph (1987), *Capitalism, Socialism and Democracy*, London: Counterpoint.

Schutz, Alfred (1962), 'On multiple realities', in Alfred Schutz, *Collected Papers I: The Problem of Social Reality*, edited by Maurice Natanson, The Hague: Martinus Nijhoff, pp. 207–259.

Schutz, Alfred (1970), *On Phenomenology and Social Relations*, edited and with an introduction by Helmut R. Wagner, Chicago, IL: University of Chicago Press.

Schwartzman, Helen (1989), *The Meeting: Gatherings in Organizations and Communities*, New York: Plenum.

Scott, John (2021), 'Constructing social structure', in Håkon Leiulfsrud & Peter Sohlberg (eds), *Constructing Social Research Objects: Constructivism in Research Practice*, Leiden: Brill, pp. 38–58.

Scott, Richard (1981), *Organizations: Rational, Natural and Open Systems*, Englewood Cliffs, NJ: Prentice Hall.

Scott, W. Richard & Gerald F. Davis (2007), *Organizations and Organizing: Rational, Natural, and Open Systems Perspectives*, Upper Saddle River, NJ: Pearson Prentice Hall.

Selznick, Philip (1948), 'Foundations of the theory of organizations', *American Sociological Review*, **13**(1), 25–35.

Shefter, Martin (1994), *Political Parties and the State: The American Historical Experience*, Princeton, NJ: Princeton University Press.

Simmel, Georg (1898), 'The persistence of social groups', *American Journal of Sociology*, **3**(5), 662–698.

Simmel, Georg (1909), 'The problem of sociology', *American Journal of Sociology*, **15**(3), 289–320.

Simmel, Georg (1950a), The Sociology of Georg Simmel, translated, edited and with an introduction by Kurt H. Wolff, New York: The Free Press.

Simmel, Georg (1910), 'How is society possible?', *American Journal of Sociology*, **16**(3), 372–391.

Simmel, Georg (1950), 'The stranger', in Kurt Wolff (ed.), *The Sociology of Georg Simmel*, New York: Free Press, pp. 402–408.

Simmel, Georg (1964), *Conflict & The Web of Group-Affiliations*, New York: Free Press.

Sklair, Leslie (1991), *Sociology of the Global System*, New York: Harvester Wheatsheaf.

Smart, Carol (2007), *Personal Life: New Directions in Sociological Thinking*, Cambridge: Polity Press.

Smith, Julie (2001), "Political parties in a global age", in Daphné Josselin & William Wallace (eds), *Non-state Actors in World Politics*, Basingstoke: Palgrave, pp. 59-75.

Spiro, Peter (2017), 'Multiple citizenship', in Ayelet Shachar, Rainer Baubäck, Irene Bloemraad & Maarten Vink (eds), *The Oxford Handbook of Citizenship*, Oxford: Oxford University Press, pp. 623–643.

Standing, Guy (2014), *The Precariat: The New Dangerous Class*, London: Bloomsbury.

Stanger, Allison (2019), *Whistleblowers: Honesty in America from Washington to Trump*, New Haven, CT: Yale University Press.

Stark, Werner (1980), *The Social Bond: An Investigation into the Bases of Law-abidingness*, Volume 3, New York: Fordham University Press.

Stearns, Peter (2020), *Globalization in World History*, 3rd edition, London: Routledge.

Stinchcombe, Arthur (1965), 'Social structure and organizations', in James March (ed.), *Handbook of Organizations*, Chicago, IL: Rand McNally, pp. 142–190.

Stinchcombe, Arthur (1968), *Constructing Social Theories*, New York: Harcourt Brace & World.

Stinchcombe, Arthur (1985), 'Macrosociology is sociology about millions of people', *Contemporary Sociology*, **14**(5), 572–575.

Stinchcombe, Arthur (1990), *Information and Organizations*, Berkeley: University of California Press.

Stone, Brad (2013), *The Everything Store: Jeff Bezos and the Age of Amazon*, London: Bantam Press.

Sugden, John Peter & Alan Tomlinson (1998), *FIFA and the Contest for World Football: Who Rules the People's Game?*, Cambridge: Polity Press.

Sundberg, Mikaela (2015), *A Sociology of the Total Organization: Atomistic Unity in the French Foreign Legion*, Farnham: Ashgate.

Sundberg, Mikaela (2019), 'Brotherhood as an organized social relationship', in Göran Ahrne & Nils Brunsson (eds), *Organization Unbound: The Abundance of Partial Organization in Social Life*, Cambridge: Cambridge University Press, pp. 271–290.

Sydow, Jörg (2019), 'The inter-firm network as partial organization?', in Göran Ahrne & Nils Brunsson (eds), *Organization Unbound: The Abundance of Partial Organization in Social Life*, Cambridge: Cambridge University Press, pp. 191–211.

Sydow, Jörg & Timo Braun (2018), 'Projects as temporary organizations: An agenda for further theorizing the interorganizational dimension', *International Journal of Project Management*, **36**(1), 4–11.

Sztompka, Piotr (1993), *The Sociology of Social Change*, Oxford: Blackwell Publishers.

Tamm Hallström, Kristina & Magnus Boström (2010), *Transnational Multi-Stakeholder Standardization: Organizing Fragile Non-State Authority*, Cheltenham, UK and Northampton, MA, USA: Edward Elgar Publishing.

Teachout, Zephyr (2014), *Corruption in America: From Benjamin Franklin's Snuff Box to Citizens United*, Cambridge, MA: Harvard University Press.

Thomas, Lawrence (2013), 'The character of friendship', in Damian Calouri (ed.), *Thinking about Friendship: Historical and Contemporary Philosophical Perspectives*, Basingstoke: Palgrave Macmillan, pp. 30–44.

Thompson, Grahame (2003), *Between Hierarchies and Markets: The Logic and Limits of Network Forms of Organization*, Oxford: Oxford University Press.

Thompson, James (1967), *Organizations in Action*, New York: McGraw-Hill.

Tilly, Charles (1984), *Big Structures, Large Processes, Huge Comparisons*, New York: Russell Sage Foundation.

Tilly, Charles (1992), *Coercion, Capital and European States: AD 990–1990*, Cambridge, MA: Basil Blackwell.

Tilly, Charles (1998), *Durable Inequality*, Berkeley: University of California Press.

Tilly, Charles (2002), *Stories, Identities and Political Change*, Berkeley: University of California Press.

Tilly, Charles (2005a), *Identities, Boundaries & Social Ties*, London: Routledge.

Tilly, Charles (2005b), *Trust and Rule*, Cambridge: Cambridge University Press.

Tilly, Charles, Louise Tilly & Richard H. Tilly (1975), *The Rebellious Century, 1830–1930*, Cambridge, MA: Harvard University Press.

Torekull, Bertil (1999), *Leading by Design: The IKEA Story*, New York: HarperCollins.

Törnqvist, Maria (2020), 'Communal intimacy: Formalization, egalitarianism and exchangeability in collective housing', *Social Forces*, doi:10.1093/sf/soaa094.

Udehn, Lars (1996), *The Limits of Public Choice: A Sociological Critique of the Economic Theory of Politics*, London: Routledge.

Udehn, Lars (2007), 'Teorier om individualisering i klassisk sociologi', in Mikael Carleheden, Rolf Lidskog & Christine Roman (eds), *Social interaktion – Förutsättningar och former*, Malmö: Liber, pp. 19–41.

Udehn, Lars (2016), 'Samhället', unpublished paper, Department of Sociology: Stockholm University.

Vandenberghe, Frederic (2018), 'The relation as magical operator: Overcoming the divide between relational and processual sociology', in Francois Dépelteau (ed.), *The Palgrave Handbook of Relational Sociology*, London: Palgrave Macmillan, pp. 35–55.

Varese, Federico (2011), *Mafias on the Move: How Organized Crime Conquers New Territories*, Princeton, NJ: Princeton University Press.

Warhurst, Chris, Diane van den Broek, Richard Hall & Dennis Nickson (2009), 'Lookism: The new frontier of employment discrimination', *Journal of Industrial Relations*, **51**(1), 131–136.

Watson, James (ed.) (1997), *Golden Arches East: McDonald's in East Asia*, Stanford, CA: Stanford University Press.

Weber, Max (1930), *The Protestant Ethic and the Spirit of Capitalism*, London: Unwin University Books.

Weber, Max (1946), 'Science as a vocation', in Hans Gerth & C. Wright Mills (eds), *From Max Weber*, New York: Oxford University Press, pp. 129–156.

Weber, Max (1968), *Economy and Society*, Volumes 1 and 2, edited by Guenther Roth & Claus Wittic, Berkeley: University of California Press.

Weeks, Jeffrey, Brian Heaphy & Catherine Donovan (2001), *Same Sex Intimacies: Families of Choice and Other Life Experiments*, London: Routledge.

Weiner, Mark S. (2013), *The Rule of the Clan: What an Ancient Form of Social Organization Reveals About the Future of Individualism*, New York: Farrar, Straus and Giroux.

Wharton, Amy (2009), 'The sociology of emotional labor', *Annual Review of Sociology*, **35**, 147–165.

White, Harrison (1992), *Identity and Control: A Structural Theory of Social Action*, Princeton, NJ: Princeton University Press.

Williamson, Oliver (1975), *Markets and Hierarchies: Analysis and Antitrust Implications: A Study in the Economics of Internal Organization*, New York: Free Press.

Williamson, Oliver (1981), 'The economics of organizations: The transaction cost approach', *American Journal of Sociology*, **87**(3), 548–577.

Winch, Peter (2008), *The Idea of a Social Science and its Relations to Philosophy*, with a new introduction by Raimond Gaita, London: Routledge.

Witz, Anne, Chris Warhurst & Dennis Nickson (2003), 'The labour of aesthetics and the aesthetics of organization', *Organization*, **10**(1), 33–54.

Young, Michael & Peter Willmott (1962), *Family and Kinship in East London*, Harmondsworth: Penguin Books.

Zaheer, Srilata (2002), 'The liability of foreignness, redux: A commentary', *Journal of International Management*, **8**(3), 351–358.

Zerubavel, Eviatar (2012), *Ancestors and Relatives: Genealogy, Identity, and Community*, Oxford: Oxford University Press.

Zuboff, Shoshana (2019), *The Age of Surveillance Capitalism: The Fight for a Human Future at the New Frontier of Power*, London: Profile Books.

Index